25 & 30HP EFI
QUICK. RELIABLE. EFFICIENT.

Mercury 25 and 30hp FourStroke outboards make light work of your biggest adventures. Quick and compact. Reliable and durable. Efficient and easy to own. FourStroke outboards bring big capabilities to small vessels.

- **Exceptionally Smooth, Quiet and Efficient**
- **Outstanding Speed and Acceleration**
- **One of the lightest 3 cylinders in class**
- **Easy to start and reliable with Battery-free EFI (Electronic Fuel Injection)**
- **Exclusive Intuitive Tiller Handle**
- **SmartCraft Capable (Electric Start Models)**
- **3+3=6 Year Fully transferable, non-declining Warranty***

*Terms and Conditions apply

mercurymarine.com.au

Contents

Using Bite Times... 4

Moon Phases... 5

Bite Time Adjustments 7

Brisbane Bar Tide Times.................................... 8 - 39

Bite Times .... 40 - 69

Townsville Tide Times .... 70 - 101

Popular Rigs... 102

Popular Knots... 103

Fish ID 104

Fish Illustrations: Trevor Hawkins

Published in 2024 by
Australian Fishing Network Pty Ltd
PO Box 544, Croydon, VIC 3136
Tel: (03) 9729 8788   Email: sales@afn.com.au   www.afn.com.au

© Copyright Australian Fishing Network 2024

ISBN 9781 8651 3429 1

DISCLAIMER

The solar/lunar bite times in this book were derived from the program WXTide32 and are predictions. While they are as accurate as possible, they should be used as a guide only. Local conditions and changes can cause variations, so consult a website such as the Bureau of Meteorology Oceanographic Services, (www. bom.gov.au/oceanography/tides) as close as possible to the tide date and time before your fishing trip for the most up-to-date information and if you require certified information.

The publisher, Australian Fishing Network, advises that the information in this guide should not be used for navigation and should not be relied on for crucial situations.

"This product is based on Bureau of Meteorology information that has subsequently been modified. The Bureau does not necessarily support or endorse, or have any connection with, the product.

In respect of that part of the information which is sourced from the Bureau, and to the maximum extent permitted by law:

(i) The Bureau makes no representation and gives no warranty of any kind whether express, implied, statutory or otherwise in respect to the availability, accuracy, currency, completeness, quality or reliability of the information or that the information will be fit for any particular purpose or will not infringe any third party Intellectual Property rights; and

(ii) the Bureau's liability for any loss, damage, cost or expense resulting from use of, or reliance on, the information is entirely excluded."

"The Bureau of Meteorology gives no warranty of any kind whether express, implied, statutory or otherwise in respect to the availability, accuracy, currency, completeness, quality or reliability of the information or that the information will be fit for any particular purpose or will not infringe any third party Intellectual Property rights. The Bureau's liability for any loss, damage, cost or expense resulting from use of, or reliance on, the information is entirely excluded."

Huk

AVAILABLE NOW

Using Bite Times

'Solunar' theory suggests all creatures great and small respond in some way to the influences of both the Sun and the Moon during the course of a day.

This book lists the peak activity times along with the moon phases and it should become an indispensable tool for when you're planning a trip.

The peak activity times are presented in this book to simulate the logical progression of the Moon as it orbits the Earth. The first is the minor peak at moonrise, no matter what time of day at which it occurs. The second is the major peak when the moon is directly overhead, the third is the minor peak at moonset and the fourth is the major peak when the moon is directly overhead on the opposite side of the globe.

Solunar (solar and lunar) theory is one of nature's mysteries which many of us find difficult to consider with any merit. A number of books, tables and articles have been written on the subject of lunar and solar influences on animal behaviour. Solunar theory suggests all creatures great and small respond in some way to the influences of both the Sun and the Moon during the course of a day. Specifically this response is often seen as an increase or decrease in activity level. Increased activity periods have often been referred to as peak or prime times.

The combination of centrifugal force produced by the Earth's rotation and the Moon's daily crossing of the sky generates our tides. Such enormous force is produced by these phenomena that it causes the Earth's surface to bulge up to 16 centimetres. Could lunar cycles impact on man? You be the judge. The human gestation period is 266 days, the average synodic interval between two consecutive new Moons is 29.530589 days; 266 divided by 29.530589 equals 9.008 lunar months. Sound familiar? Man is made up of approximately 80 per cent water. We know what happens tidally to huge bodies of water. Do you think there is a remote possibility that we too could unknowingly experience the effects of this heavenly sphere?

It is important to understand that what influences one creature may not influence another in any circumstance. For example there are a number of intertidal organisms that are most active when submerged by an incoming tide, creatures such as barnacles, green crabs, snails, clams, and oysters. Others, like soldier crabs and shorebirds, are especially adapted to feed on beaches exposed at low tide. The lower the creature's order in the animal kingdom the more likely it is to respond to solar and lunar stimuli.

LIGHT THEORY

The light theory suggests that light levels during the day and night dictate feeding activity times. For example it is said that fishing is better on the mornings immediately leading up to and following the period of new Moon because the fish have been unable to feed during the periods of low light during the night. Fishing is also said to be good during the nights leading up to and following the full Moon because of increased evening light levels.

SOLAR THEORY

To some extent the solar theory is reliant upon seasonal changes, therefore I have provided you with a brief summary of the seasonal patterns and how they influence the Southern Hemisphere.

The principle of the solar theory works on the various instances of the Sun's rise, upper transit, set, and lower transit to identify the peak activity periods. Following a long period of darkness the animal kingdom is given a kick-start to the day as dawn approaches. Many creatures stir from their rest period and warm with the Sun to commence the daily routine of food gathering. All animal life has a preferred temperature range and fish are no exception to this rule. It is said that seasonal conditions may dictate when particular fish species will commence to feed.

So although dawn and dusk have been historically noted as prime fishing times if we review the seasonal fluctuations in day and night time temperatures we may see cause for reassessing our reliance on these times. For example during the colder months peak feeding times may coincide during the warmest time of the day; just after midday when the water temperatures have increased to a more preferred level. Conversely, during the warmer months peak feeding times may align with the coolest times of the day; dusk 'til dawn.

SEASONS

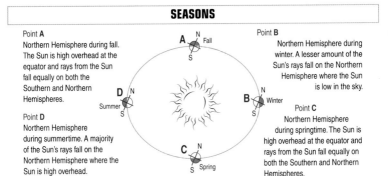

Point A
Northern Hemisphere during fall. The Sun is high overhead at the equator and rays from the Sun fall equally on both the Southern and Northern Hemispheres.

Point D
Northern Hemisphere during summertime. A majority of the Sun's rays fall on the Northern Hemisphere where the Sun is high overhead.

Point B
Northern Hemisphere during winter. A lesser amount of the Sun's rays fall on the Northern Hemisphere where the Sun is low in the sky.

Point C
Northern Hemisphere during springtime. The Sun is high overhead at the equator and rays from the Sun fall equally on both the Southern and Northern Hemispheres.

LUNAR THEORY

To help you understand the lunar theory in more depth I have provided a brief outline of the various lunar phases. When you watch the Moon over a course of several days you will see that its appearance changes. The varying appearances called 'phases' depend upon the relative positions of the Sun and Moon.

MOON PHASES

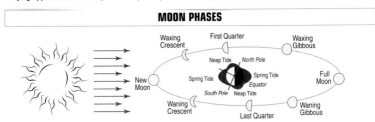

NEW MOON

When the Moon is between the Sun and the Earth we cannot see any of the illuminated side of the Moon, the Moon is dark, we call this phase the new Moon and it is the beginning of a new lunar month. The Moon rises and sets with the Sun during the new Moon. The gravitational forces exerted on the Earth by the Moon and the Sun is greatest at this time. The first of the spring tides for the lunar month occurs during this period.

FULL MOON

As the illuminated portion grows we have a waxing gibbous Moon. The full Moon occurs when the Moon reaches the side of the Earth opposite from the Sun. It appears large and bright. The Moon rises as the Sun is setting—it is overhead about midnight and sets close to dawn. The gravitational forces on the Earth have increased since the first quarter and now the combined pull of the Moon and the Sun is at a maximum again for the lunar month, the second of the spring tides occur.

FIRST QUARTER

The amount of lighted surface visible from the Earth begins to grow and we see a waxing crescent Moon. When the Moon reaches the first quarter we see half of it lit. The Moon rises during the middle of the day and is overhead about dusk and sets around midnight. The Moon's illuminated side will appear on the right in the Northern Hemisphere. The gravitational forces on the Earth have reduced since the new Moon and now the combined pull of the Moon and the Sun is at a minimum for the lunar month. The first of the neap tides for the Lunar month occurs at this time.

LAST QUARTER

The gravitational forces on the Earth have reduced since the full Moon and now the combined pull of the Moon and the Sun is at a minimum again for the lunar month. The second of the neap tides for the lunar month occurs at this time. As a waning crescent, the Moon diminishes to a thin sliver, returning to a new Moon after approximately 29.5 solar days or one lunar month. As the Moon revolves around the Earth it rotates on its own axis at the same rate it revolves, therefore the Moon always keeps the same face toward the Earth.

TIDAL FORCES

As the Earth rotates on its axis once every 24 hours relative to the Sun, and 24 hours and 53 minutes relative to the Moon; the Moon rises approximately 53 minutes later with respect to the Sun each day. This delay or lagging can be seen in the variation of tides from day to day.

The principle of the lunar theory works on the various instances of the Moon's rise, upper transit, set, and lower transit to identify the peak activity periods. This theory can also take into account the various lunar phases and the proximity (apogee and perigee) of the Moon to the Earth during the period of one lunation (new Moon to new Moon). Because the Moon orbits the Earth on an elliptical path, the distance between the two is always changing. The Moon has less gravitational influence on the Earth around the time of apogee when the distance between the two bodies is at a maximum. Greater gravitational influence occurs around the time of perigee when the distance between the Earth and the Moon is at a minimum.

SOLUNAR THEORY

Solunar theory accounts for the peaks associated with both the solar and lunar theories. It also incorporates the Sun's lower transit (midnight), and it also flags the coinciding times of peaks from the other theories. In other words it takes an each way bet on the three individual theories. Additionally the solunar theory recognises the gravitational effect on the Earth from the combined force produced by the Moon and the Sun in tandem. This gravitational force changes with the seasons, with the phases of the Moon, and with the Sun and Moon's proximity to Earth.

EFFECTS ON FISHING

Fishing wise, catch rates are often said to be higher around the new and full Moon phases. This makes sense when you consider the increased gravitational influence on the Earth during these periods. However this is further bolstered if you consider that during these times we are provided with three windows of peak activity level during general daylight hours, each coinciding with dawn, noon, or dusk. Around the period of new Moon, the Moon is in harmony with the Sun, they rise, transit and set together. During the period of full Moon, the Moon and Sun directly oppose each other, the Moon sets when the Sun rises, the Moon is underfoot at noon, and the Moon rises at Sun set. Whether or not the increased activity levels in lower organisms is the catalyst for larger and perhaps predatory creatures to begin feeding is arguable. Your observations will also show increased activity levels in the non predatory herbivore family during the peak times.

FEEDING PATTERNS

Does activity occur outside of these peak periods? Of course. Remember not all species will react in an identical manner during the peak times. The bottom line is fish don't always feel hungry! They follow certain feeding patterns but aren't totally immune to sampling the odd tid-bit throughout the course of the day. As with most creatures, strength is gained through struggle; and only the fittest and strongest survive in the wild. While minimum work for maximum return is the hallmark of big fish, a fish's condition and health must also be maintained through foraging for food. Natural rhythms aside, fish are also subject to local conditions such as the various fluctuations in air temperature, barometric pressure, water levels, water clarity, and water temperature. These should all be considered when using the tables.

 BITE TIME ADJUSTMENTS (Minutes)

Approximate variation times only, taken from various sources.

BITE TIMES

Brisbane	-30		Hervey Bay	-30
Burketown	+30		Longreach	0
Cairns	0		Mackay	-20
Cape York	+10		Mount Isa	+30
Cloncurry	+30		Normanton	+20
Emerald	-10		Rockhampton	-20
Gladstone	-25		Toowoomba	-30
Gold Coast	-30		Townsville	-5
Goondawindi	-25		Weipa	+10

TIDE TIMES

Tim Smith's

POPULAR TIDE ADJUSTMENTS

Ballina	-1hr 10min
Bribie Island	-10min
Brunswick Heads	-1hr 20min
Bundaberg	-55min
Burleigh Heads	-1hr 30 min
Byron Bay	-1hr 20min
Caloundra	-1hr 25min
Cleveland	+15min
Coomera River	+1hr 30min
Donnybrook	+1hr
Fraser Island East	-1hr 20min
Gladstone	-20min
Gold Coast Seaway	-1hr 15min
Hervey Bay	+1hr
Jumpinpin	-1hr 30min
Manly	+15min
Mooloolaba	-1hr 20min
Nerang River	+1hr
Noosa	-1hr 30min
Point Danger	-1hr 30min
Redcliffe	0
Redland Bay	+30min
Runaway Bay	-30min
Sanctuary Cove	+30min
Scarborough	+5min
Southport Broadwater	-35min
Tangalooma	-30min
Tin Can Bay	-45min
Toorbul	+30min
Tweed Heads	-45min
Urngan	-45min
Victoria Pt	+15min
Brunswick Heads	- 11hr 15min
Cabbage Tree Pt	+ 30min
Cape Moreton	- 1hr 15min
Jacobs Well	+ 14min
Peel Island	+12min
Rainbow Beach	- 1hr 20min
Tallebudgera Bridge	- 1hr 18min
Tewantin	- 15min

Brisbane Bar

Day	Date		Tide 1	
Sun	1		2:56 AM	(0.52) L
Mon	2		3:30 AM	(0.50) L
Tue	3	●	4:00 AM	(0.49) L
Wed	4		4:26 AM	(0.47) L
THu	5		4:50 AM	(0.45) L
Fri	6		5:15 AM	(0.44) L
Sat	7		5:41 AM	(0.45) L
Sun	8		6:07 AM	(0.49) L
Mon	9		12:15 AM	(1.81) H
Tue	10		12:50 AM	(1.66) H
Wed	11		1:41 AM	(1.51) H
THu	12		3:04 AM	(1.42) H
Fri	13		4:45 AM	(1.45) H
Sat	14		12:37 AM	(0.74) L
Sun	15		1:32 AM	(0.57) L
Mon	16		2:21 AM	(0.43) L
Tue	17		3:05 AM	(0.31) L
Wed	18	○	3:45 AM	(0.23) L
THu	19		4:25 AM	(0.18) L
Fri	20		5:00 AM	(0.18) L
Sat	21		5:35 AM	(0.22) L
Sun	22		6:10 AM	(0.30) L
Mon	23		12:34 AM	(1.79) H
Tue	24		1:28 AM	(1.57) H
Wed	25		2:45 AM	(1.41) H
THu	26		4:30 AM	(1.39) H
Fri	27		12:12 AM	(0.74) L
Sat	28		1:03 AM	(0.64) L
Sun	29		1:45 AM	(0.55) L
Mon	30		2:19 AM	(0.49) L

SEPTEMBER 2024

Tide 2	Tide 3	Tide 4
8:32 AM (1.80) H	2:30 PM (0.44) L	8:50 PM (2.37) H
9:08 AM (1.87) H	3:08 PM (0.42) L	9:24 PM (2.36) H
9:41 AM (1.92) H	3:43 PM (0.43) L	9:55 PM (2.34) H
10:12 AM (1.97) H	4:15 PM (0.45) L	10:23 PM (2.29) H
10:43 AM (2.01) H	4:48 PM (0.50) L	10:49 PM (2.21) H
11:15 AM (2.03) H	5:22 PM (0.57) L	11:16 PM (2.10) H
11:49 AM (2.04) H	5:58 PM (0.67) L	11:45 PM (1.97) H
12:25 PM (2.01) H	6:35 PM (0.78) L	
6:36 AM (0.55) L	1:05 PM (1.97) H	7:20 PM (0.88) L
7:10 AM (0.62) L	1:54 PM (1.93) H	8:19 PM (0.97) L
7:59 AM (0.70) L	3:01 PM (1.92) H	9:47 PM (0.99) L
9:13 AM (0.74) L	4:27 PM (1.97) H	11:25 PM (0.89) L
10:41 AM (0.70) L	5:43 PM (2.12) H	
6:02 AM (1.58) H	11:56 AM (0.58) L	6:44 PM (2.29) H
7:02 AM (1.74) H	1:00 PM (0.44) L	7:35 PM (2.45) H
7:54 AM (1.91) H	1:58 PM (0.32) L	8:22 PM (2.56) H
8:43 AM (2.05) H	2:51 PM (0.24) L	9:06 PM (2.60) H
9:30 AM (2.18) H	3:42 PM (0.21) L	9:47 PM (2.57) H
10:15 AM (2.29) H	4:30 PM (0.23) L	10:29 PM (2.46) H
11:00 AM (2.36) H	5:18 PM (0.32) L	11:09 PM (2.27) H
11:46 AM (2.38) H	6:07 PM (0.46) L	11:50 PM (2.04) H
12:34 PM (2.34) H	7:00 PM (0.62) L	
6:47 AM (0.42) L	1:27 PM (2.26) H	8:04 PM (0.77) L
7:31 AM (0.56) L	2:29 PM (2.16) H	9:29 PM (0.85) L
8:34 AM (0.69) L	3:44 PM (2.09) H	11:00 PM (0.83) L
10:02 AM (0.76) L	5:02 PM (2.09) H	
5:49 AM (1.50) H	11:29 AM (0.72) L	6:07 PM (2.14) H
6:45 AM (1.65) H	12:34 PM (0.64) L	6:59 PM (2.19) H
7:30 AM (1.79) H	1:26 PM (0.55) L	7:41 PM (2.23) H
8:07 AM (1.90) H	2:08 PM (0.50) L	8:17 PM (2.25) H

TIDE TIMES

Tim Smith's

POPULAR TIDE ADJUSTMENTS

Ballina	-1hr 10min
Bribie Island	-10min
Brunswick Heads	-1hr 20min
Bundaberg	-55min
Burleigh Heads	-1hr 30 min
Byron Bay	-1hr 20min
Caloundra	-1hr 25min
Cleveland	+15min
Coomera River	+1hr 30min
Donnybrook	+1hr
Fraser Island East	-1hr 20min
Gladstone	-20min
Gold Coast Seaway	-1hr 15min
Hervey Bay	+1hr
Jumpinpin	-1hr 30min
Manly	+15min
Mooloolaba	-1hr 20min
Nerang River	+1hr
Noosa	-1hr 30min
Point Danger	-1hr 30min
Redcliffe	0
Redland Bay	+30min
Runaway Bay	-30min
Sanctuary Cove	+30min
Scarborough	+5min
Southport Broadwater	-35min
Tangalooma	-30min
Tin Can Bay	-45min
Toorbul	+30min
Tweed Heads	-45min
Urngan	-45min
Victoria Pt	+15min
Brunswick Heads	- 11hr 15min
Cabbage Tree Pt	+ 30min
Cape Moreton	- 1hr 15min
Jacobs Well	+ 14min
Peel Island	+12min
Rainbow Beach	- 1hr 20min
Tallebudgera Bridge	- 1hr 18min
Tewantin	- 15min

Brisbane Bar

Day	Date		Tide 1	
Tue	1		2:50 AM	(0.45) L
Wed	2		3:18 AM	(0.41) L
THu	3	●	3:44 AM	(0.38) L
Fri	4		4:09 AM	(0.36) L
Sat	5		4:35 AM	(0.37) L
Sun	6		5:00 AM	(0.40) L
Mon	7		5:28 AM	(0.46) L
Tue	8		5:57 AM	(0.53) L
Wed	9		12:28 AM	(1.57) H
THu	10		1:23 AM	(1.47) H
Fri	11		2:50 AM	(1.42) H
Sat	12		4:29 AM	(1.49) H
Sun	13		12:03 AM	(0.65) L
Mon	14		12:58 AM	(0.49) L
Tue	15		1:46 AM	(0.35) L
Wed	16		2:30 AM	(0.24) L
THu	17	○	3:10 AM	(0.17) L
Fri	18		3:47 AM	(0.14) L
Sat	19		4:24 AM	(0.16) L
Sun	20		4:59 AM	(0.22) L
Mon	21		5:35 AM	(0.33) L
Tue	22		12:19 AM	(1.63) H
Wed	23		1:17 AM	(1.48) H
THu	24		2:36 AM	(1.40) H
Fri	25		4:06 AM	(1.43) H
Sat	26		5:18 AM	(1.55) H
Sun	27		12:17 AM	(0.65) L
Mon	28		12:58 AM	(0.56) L
Tue	29		1:32 AM	(0.49) L
Wed	30		2:04 AM	(0.42) L
THu	31		2:34 AM	(0.38) L

Tide 2		Tide 3		Tide 4	
8:41 AM	(1.99) **H**	2:46 PM	(0.47) L	8:50 PM	(2.24) **H**
9:14 AM	(2.06) **H**	3:22 PM	(0.47) L	9:20 PM	(2.20) **H**
9:45 AM	(2.13) **H**	3:58 PM	(0.49) L	9:48 PM	(2.14) **H**
10:16 AM	(2.17) **H**	4:32 PM	(0.53) L	10:16 PM	(2.05) **H**
10:48 AM	(2.19) **H**	5:06 PM	(0.59) L	10:45 PM	(1.94) **H**
11:22 AM	(2.18) **H**	5:42 PM	(0.67) L	11:15 PM	(1.82) **H**
11:57 AM	(2.15) **H**	6:20 PM	(0.76) L	11:47 PM	(1.69) **H**
12:35 PM	(2.10) **H**	7:04 PM	(0.84) L		
6:32 AM	(0.61) L	1:23 PM	(2.04) **H**	8:03 PM	(0.90) L
7:24 AM	(0.70) L	2:27 PM	(2.01) **H**	9:29 PM	(0.90) L
8:42 AM	(0.75) L	3:47 PM	(2.05) **H**	10:56 PM	(0.80) L
10:12 AM	(0.71) L	5:04 PM	(2.16) **H**		
5:43 AM	(1.66) **H**	11:30 AM	(0.60) L	6:07 PM	(2.29) **H**
6:42 AM	(1.86) **H**	12:38 PM	(0.48) L	7:00 PM	(2.40) **H**
7:33 AM	(2.06) **H**	1:39 PM	(0.38) L	7:49 PM	(2.44) **H**
8:22 AM	(2.23) **H**	2:35 PM	(0.32) L	8:34 PM	(2.42) **H**
9:08 AM	(2.37) **H**	3:28 PM	(0.30) L	9:18 PM	(2.34) **H**
9:54 AM	(2.48) **H**	4:19 PM	(0.33) L	10:01 PM	(2.20) **H**
10:40 AM	(2.53) **H**	5:09 PM	(0.40) L	10:45 PM	(2.02) **H**
11:26 AM	(2.52) **H**	6:01 PM	(0.51) L	11:30 PM	(1.82) **H**
12:14 PM	(2.45) **H**	6:57 PM	(0.63) L		
6:14 AM	(0.47) L	1:04 PM	(2.33) **H**	8:01 PM	(0.74) L
7:00 AM	(0.62) L	2:00 PM	(2.20) **H**	9:15 PM	(0.80) L
8:02 AM	(0.76) L	3:07 PM	(2.09) **H**	10:27 PM	(0.79) L
9:30 AM	(0.84) L	4:18 PM	(2.04) **H**	11:28 PM	(0.73) L
10:55 AM	(0.82) L	5:22 PM	(2.05) **H**		
6:14 AM	(1.71) **H**	12:00 PM	(0.75) L	6:14 PM	(2.07) **H**
6:58 AM	(1.86) **H**	12:53 PM	(0.68) L	6:58 PM	(2.09) **H**
7:36 AM	(1.99) **H**	1:39 PM	(0.62) L	7:36 PM	(2.10) **H**
8:12 AM	(2.11) **H**	2:21 PM	(0.58) L	8:11 PM	(2.07) **H**
8:45 AM	(2.20) **H**	3:01 PM	(0.56) L	8:44 PM	(2.03) **H**

TIDE TIMES

Tim Smith's

POPULAR TIDE ADJUSTMENTS

Ballina	-1hr 10min
Bribie Island	-10min
Brunswick Heads	-1hr 20min
Bundaberg	-55min
Burleigh Heads	-1hr 30 min
Byron Bay	-1hr 20min
Caloundra	-1hr 25min
Cleveland	+15min
Coomera River	+1hr 30min
Donnybrook	+1hr
Fraser Island East	-1hr 20min
Gladstone	-20min
Gold Coast Seaway	-1hr 15min
Hervey Bay	+1hr
Jumpinpin	-1hr 30min
Manly	+15min
Mooloolaba	-1hr 20min
Nerang River	+1hr
Noosa	-1hr 30min
Point Danger	-1hr 30min
Redcliffe	0
Redland Bay	+30min
Runaway Bay	-30min
Sanctuary Cove	+30min
Scarborough	+5min
Southport Broadwater	-35min
Tangalooma	-30min
Tin Can Bay	-45min
Toorbul	+30min
Tweed Heads	-45min
Urngan	-45min
Victoria Pt	+15min
Brunswick Heads	- 11hr 15min
Cabbage Tree Pt	+ 30min
Cape Moreton	- 1hr 15min
Jacobs Well	+ 14min
Peel Island	+12min
Rainbow Beach	- 1hr 20min
Tallebudgera Bridge	- 1hr 18min
Tewantin	- 15min

Brisbane Bar

Day	Date		Tide 1	
Fri	1 ●	3:03 AM	(0.34)	L
Sat	2	3:31 AM	(0.34)	L
Sun	3	4:00 AM	(0.35)	L
Mon	4	4:29 AM	(0.39)	L
Tue	5	5:00 AM	(0.44)	L
Wed	6	5:32 AM	(0.51)	L
THu	7	12:20 AM	(1.57)	H
Fri	8	1:20 AM	(1.52)	H
Sat	9	2:40 AM	(1.52)	H
Sun	10	4:04 AM	(1.61)	H
Mon	11	5:16 AM	(1.79)	H
Tue	12	12:16 AM	(0.44)	L
Wed	13	1:06 AM	(0.32)	L
THu	14	1:51 AM	(0.24)	L
Fri	15	2:33 AM	(0.19)	L
Sat	16 ○	3:13 AM	(0.18)	L
Sun	17	3:52 AM	(0.21)	L
Mon	18	4:30 AM	(0.28)	L
Tue	19	5:09 AM	(0.38)	L
Wed	20	12:07 AM	(1.60)	H
THu	21	1:01 AM	(1.53)	H
Fri	22	2:03 AM	(1.49)	H
Sat	23	3:15 AM	(1.52)	H
Sun	24	4:26 AM	(1.60)	H
Mon	25	5:27 AM	(1.74)	H
Tue	26	6:17 AM	(1.89)	H
Wed	27	12:38 AM	(0.53)	L
THu	28	1:15 AM	(0.46)	L
Fri	29	1:51 AM	(0.41)	L
Sat	30	2:26 AM	(0.38)	L

NOVEMBER 2024

Tide 2		Tide 3		Tide 4	
9:19 AM	(2.27) H	3:40 PM	(0.56) L	9:15 PM	(1.97) H
9:52 AM	(2.31) H	4:17 PM	(0.58) L	9:47 PM	(1.89) H
10:26 AM	(2.33) H	4:55 PM	(0.62) L	10:20 PM	(1.81) H
11:00 AM	(2.31) H	5:32 PM	(0.67) L	10:55 PM	(1.73) H
11:37 AM	(2.28) H	6:14 PM	(0.73) L	11:34 PM	(1.64) H
12:18 PM	(2.23) H	7:00 PM	(0.78) L		
6:15 AM	(0.59) L	1:06 PM	(2.19) H	8:00 PM	(0.81) L
7:10 AM	(0.66) L	2:06 PM	(2.17) H	9:11 PM	(0.78) L
8:22 AM	(0.72) L	3:14 PM	(2.17) H	10:20 PM	(0.69) L
9:45 AM	(0.71) L	4:22 PM	(2.21) H	11:21 PM	(0.57) L
11:03 AM	(0.65) L	5:25 PM	(2.26) H		
6:16 AM	(1.99) H	12:15 PM	(0.58) L	6:22 PM	(2.27) H
7:11 AM	(2.20) H	1:20 PM	(0.51) L	7:15 PM	(2.24) H
8:00 AM	(2.38) H	2:21 PM	(0.46) L	8:04 PM	(2.17) H
8:49 AM	(2.51) H	3:17 PM	(0.44) L	8:52 PM	(2.06) H
9:36 AM	(2.60) H	4:12 PM	(0.44) L	9:41 PM	(1.94) H
10:22 AM	(2.63) H	5:04 PM	(0.48) L	10:29 PM	(1.82) H
11:08 AM	(2.59) H	5:57 PM	(0.55) L	11:17 PM	(1.70) H
11:55 AM	(2.50) H	6:50 PM	(0.63) L		
5:50 AM	(0.50) L	12:42 PM	(2.38) H	7:44 PM	(0.70) L
6:36 AM	(0.64) L	1:30 PM	(2.25) H	8:38 PM	(0.75) L
7:31 AM	(0.77) L	2:22 PM	(2.13) H	9:31 PM	(0.77) L
8:41 AM	(0.86) L	3:18 PM	(2.05) H	10:24 PM	(0.74) L
9:59 AM	(0.90) L	4:16 PM	(1.99) H	11:14 PM	(0.68) L
11:10 AM	(0.89) L	5:13 PM	(1.96) H	11:58 PM	(0.60) L
12:13 PM	(0.84) L	6:02 PM	(1.94) H		
7:01 AM	(2.04) H	1:07 PM	(0.78) L	6:47 PM	(1.92) H
7:41 AM	(2.17) H	1:56 PM	(0.72) L	7:30 PM	(1.89) H
8:18 AM	(2.28) H	2:41 PM	(0.67) L	8:09 PM	(1.86) H
8:56 AM	(2.36) H	3:24 PM	(0.64) L	8:47 PM	(1.82) H

TIDE TIMES

Tim Smith's

POPULAR TIDE ADJUSTMENTS

Ballina	-1hr 10min
Bribie Island	-10min
Brunswick Heads	-1hr 20min
Bundaberg	-55min
Burleigh Heads	-1hr 30 min
Byron Bay	-1hr 20min
Caloundra	-1hr 25min
Cleveland	+15min
Coomera River	+1hr 30min
Donnybrook	+1hr
Fraser Island East	-1hr 20min
Gladstone	-20min
Gold Coast Seaway	-1hr 15min
Hervey Bay	+1hr
Jumpinpin	-1hr 30min
Manly	+15min
Mooloolaba	-1hr 20min
Nerang River	+1hr
Noosa	-1hr 30min
Point Danger	-1hr 30min
Redcliffe	0
Redland Bay	+30min
Runaway Bay	-30min
Sanctuary Cove	+30min
Scarborough	+5min
Southport Broadwater	-35min
Tangalooma	-30min
Tin Can Bay	-45min
Toorbul	+30min
Tweed Heads	-45min
Urngan	-45min
Victoria Pt	+15min
Brunswick Heads	- 11hr 15min
Cabbage Tree Pt	+ 30min
Cape Moreton	- 1hr 15min
Jacobs Well	+ 14min
Peel Island	+12min
Rainbow Beach	- 1hr 20min
Tallebudgera Bridge	- 1hr 18min
Tewantin	- 15min

Brisbane Bar

Day	Date		Tide 1	
Sun	1 ●	3:00 AM	(0.36)	L
Mon	2	3:32 AM	(0.37)	L
Tue	3	4:07 AM	(0.39)	L
Wed	4	4:43 AM	(0.42)	L
THu	5	5:22 AM	(0.46)	L
Fri	6	12:19 AM	(1.67)	H
Sat	7	1:15 AM	(1.66)	H
Sun	8	2:22 AM	(1.69)	H
Mon	9	3:35 AM	(1.77)	H
Tue	10	4:46 AM	(1.91)	H
Wed	11	5:51 AM	(2.10)	H
THu	12	12:24 AM	(0.37)	L
Fri	13	1:15 AM	(0.32)	L
Sat	14	2:02 AM	(0.29)	L
Sun	15 ○	2:48 AM	(0.28)	L
Mon	16	3:31.AM	(0.30)	L
Tue	17	4:14 AM	(0.34)	L
Wed	18	4:54 AM	(0.41)	L
THu	19	5:34 AM	(0.50)	L
Fri	20	12:34 AM	(1.67)	H
Sat	21	1:20 AM	(1.65)	H
Sun	22	2:12 AM	(1.65)	H
Mon	23	3:15 AM	(1.68)	H
Tue	24	4:24 AM	(1.76)	H
Wed	25	5:29 AM	(1.88)	H
THu	26	6:23 AM	(2.03)	H
Fri	27	12:27 AM	(0.56)	L
Sat	28	1:12 AM	(0.51)	L
Sun	29	1:54 AM	(0.46)	L
Mon	30	2:35 AM	(0.42)	L
Tue	31 ●	3:15 AM	(0.38)	L

Tide 2		Tide 3		Tide 4	
9:32 AM	(2.40) **H**	4:06 PM	(0.63) L	9:25 PM	(1.79) **H**
10:09 AM	(2.42) **H**	4:46 PM	(0.64) L	10:04 PM	(1.76) **H**
10:46 AM	(2.43) **H**	5:29 PM	(0.65) L	10:45 PM	(1.73) **H**
11:27 AM	(2.41) **H**	6:13 PM	(0.67) L	11:30 PM	(1.70) **H**
12:09 PM	(2.39) **H**	7:00 PM	(0.69) L		
6:08 AM	(0.53) L	12:55 PM	(2.36) **H**	7:50 PM	(0.68) L
7:02 AM	(0.60) L	1:45 PM	(2.33) **H**	8:45 PM	(0.65) L
8:06 AM	(0.67) L	2:41 PM	(2.28) **H**	9:40 PM	(0.59) L
9:20 AM	(0.73) L	3:41 PM	(2.22) **H**	10:36 PM	(0.52) L
10:36 AM	(0.74) L	4:44 PM	(2.15) **H**	11:30 PM	(0.44) L
11:53 AM	(0.72) L	5:45 PM	(2.07) **H**		
6:50 AM	(2.28) **H**	1:08 PM	(0.67) L	6:45 PM	(1.98) **H**
7:44 AM	(2.45) **H**	2:15 PM	(0.61) L	7:42 PM	(1.90) **H**
8:34 AM	(2.56) **H**	3:15 PM	(0.56) L	8:38 PM	(1.84) **H**
9:23 AM	(2.63) **H**	4:09 PM	(0.53) L	9:30 PM	(1.79) **H**
10:09 AM	(2.64) **H**	5:00 PM	(0.54) L	10:20 PM	(1.75) **H**
10:54 AM	(2.60) **H**	5:47 PM	(0.57) L	11:07 PM	(1.72) **H**
11:36 AM	(2.52) **H**	6:30 PM	(0.62) L	11:51 PM	(1.69) **H**
12:16 PM	(2.42) **H**	7:11 PM	(0.67) L		
6:15 AM	(0.61) L	12:56 PM	(2.31) **H**	7:49 PM	(0.71) L
7:00 AM	(0.72) L	1:36 PM	(2.20) **H**	8:29 PM	(0.72) L
7:52 AM	(0.84) L	2:18 PM	(2.08) **H**	9:11 PM	(0.72) !
8:55 AM	(0.94) L	3:06 PM	(1.97) **H**	9:58 PM	(0.70) L
10:08 AM	(1.00) L	4:01 PM	(1.87) **H**	10:48 PM	(0.66) L
11:25 AM	(0.99) L	5:00 PM	(1.79) **H**	11:38 PM	(0.62) L
12:33 PM	(0.93) L	5:59 PM	(1.75) **H**		
7:10 AM	(2.17) **H**	1:32 PM	(0.84) L	6:52 PM	(1.73) **H**
7:53 AM	(2.29) **H**	2:23 PM	(0.76) L	7:41 PM	(1.73) **H**
8:35 AM	(2.38) **H**	3:10 PM	(0.69) L	8:27 PM	(1.75) **H**
9:15 AM	(2.45) **H**	3:55 PM	(0.65) L	9:11 PM	(1.77) **H**
9:55 AM	(2.51) **H**	4:38 PM	(0.62) L	9:55 PM	(1.80) **H**

TIDE TIMES

Tim Smith's

Brisbane Bar

POPULAR TIDE ADJUSTMENTS

Ballina	-1hr 10min
Bribie Island	-10min
Brunswick Heads	-1hr 20min
Bundaberg	-55min
Burleigh Heads	-1hr 30 min
Byron Bay	-1hr 20min
Caloundra	-1hr 25min
Cleveland	+15min
Coomera River	+1hr 30min
Donnybrook	+1hr
Fraser Island East	-1hr 20min
Gladstone	-20min
Gold Coast Seaway	-1hr 15min
Hervey Bay	+1hr
Jumpinpin	-1hr 30min
Manly	+15min
Mooloolaba	-1hr 20min
Nerang River	+1hr
Noosa	-1hr 30min
Point Danger	-1hr 30min
Redcliffe	0
Redland Bay	+30min
Runaway Bay	-30min
Sanctuary Cove	+30min
Scarborough	+5min
Southport Broadwater	-35min
Tangalooma	-30min
Tin Can Bay	-45min
Toorbul	+30min
Tweed Heads	-45min
Urngan	-45min
Victoria Pt	+15min
Brunswick Heads	- 11hr 15min
Cabbage Tree Pt	+ 30min
Cape Moreton	- 1hr 15min
Jacobs Well	+ 14min
Peel Island	+12min
Rainbow Beach	- 1hr 20min
Tallebudgera Bridge	- 1hr 18min
Tewantin	- 15min

Day	Date	Tide 1	
Wed	1	3:55 AM	(0.37) L
THu	2	4:36 AM	(0.37) L
Fri	3	5:18 AM	(0.39) L
Sat	4	12:12 AM	(1.87) H
Sun	5	1:03 AM	(1.88) H
Mon	6	1:59 AM	(1.90) H
Tue	7	3:03 AM	(1.95) H
Wed	8	4:15 AM	(2.04) H
THu	9	5:27 AM	(2.17) H
Fri	10	6:33 AM	(2.31) H
Sat	11	12:48 AM	(0.47) L
Sun	12	1:45 AM	(0.43) L
Mon	13	2:37 AM	(0.40) L
Tue	14 ○	3:23 AM	(0.38) L
Wed	15	4:04 AM	(0.39) L
THu	16	4:43 AM	(0.43) L
Fri	17	5:18 AM	(0.50) L
Sat	18	12:03 AM	(1.86) H
Sun	19	12:40 AM	(1.86) H
Mon	20	1:21 AM	(1.85) H
Tue	21	2:10 AM	(1.84) H
Wed	22	3:10 AM	(1.84) H
THu	23	4:24 AM	(1.89) H
Fri	24	5:37 AM	(1.99) H
Sat	25	6:37 AM	(2.12) H
Sun	26	12:35 AM	(0.65) L
Mon	27	1:29 AM	(0.56) L
Tue	28	2:16 AM	(0.47) L
Wed	29 ●	3:02 AM	(0.39) L
THu	30	3:46 AM	(0.33) L
Fri	31	4:30 AM	(0.31) L

Tide 2		Tide 3		Tide 4	
10:35 AM	(2.55) H	5:21 PM	(0.60) L	10:39 PM	(1.84) H
11:15 AM	(2.57) H	6:03 PM	(0.58) L	11:25 PM	(1.86) H
11:56 AM	(2.56) H	6:45 PM	(0.57) L		
6:04 AM	(0.46) L	12:37 PM	(2.51) H	7:27 PM	(0.56) L
6:54 AM	(0.55) L	1:21 PM	(2.42) H	8:10 PM	(0.55) L
7:51 AM	(0.67) L	2:08 PM	(2.28) H	8:57 PM	(0.55) L
8:58 AM	(0.78) L	3:02 PM	(2.12) H	9:48 PM	(0.54) L
10:15 AM	(0.86) L	4:06 PM	(1.96) H	10:45 PM	(0.52) L
11:42 AM	(0.87) L	5:16 PM	(1.83) H	11:46 PM	(0.50) L
1:06 PM	(0.81) L	6:30 PM	(1.75) H		
7:32 AM	(2.45) H	2:16 PM	(0.71) L	7:38 PM	(1.74) H
8:26 AM	(2.54) H	3:14 PM	(0.63) L	8:37 PM	(1.76) H
9:14 AM	(2.60) H	4:04 PM	(0.58) L	9:27 PM	(1.79) H
9:57 AM	(2.60) H	4:47 PM	(0.58) L	10:11 PM	(1.82) H
10:37 AM	(2.58) H	5:25 PM	(0.59) L	10:50 PM	(1.84) H
11:14 AM	(2.52) H	5:59 PM	(0.62) L	11:28 PM	(1.85) H
11:47 AM	(2.44) H	6:29 PM	(0.64) L		
5:54 AM	(0.58) L	12:19 PM	(2.35) H	6:58 PM	(0.65) L
6:31 AM	(0.69) L	12:51 PM	(2.23) H	7:27 PM	(0.66) L
7:14 AM	(0.82) L	1:25 PM	(2.09) H	8:00 PM	(0.68) L
8:04 AM	(0.95) L	2:04 PM	(1.93) H	8:42 PM	(0.71) L
9:10 AM	(1.05) L	2:54 PM	(1.78) H	9:32 PM	(0.74) L
10:32 AM	(1.09) L	4:00 PM	(1.66) H	10:33 PM	(0.75) L
12:00 PM	(1.04) L	5:14 PM	(1.61) H	11:37 PM	(0.72) L
1:10 PM	(0.93) L	6:23 PM	(1.62) H		
7:28 AM	(2.26) H	2:05 PM	(0.82) L	7:21 PM	(1.69) H
8:14 AM	(2.39) H	2:54 PM	(0.72) L	8:12 PM	(1.77) H
8:57 AM	(2.50) H	3:38 PM	(0.63) L	8:59 PM	(1.85) H
9:38 AM	(2.59) H	4:21 PM	(0.56) L	9:44 PM	(1.94) H
10:18 AM	(2.65) H	5:01 PM	(0.51) L	10:29 PM	(2.01) H
10:58 AM	(2.67) H	5:41 PM	(0.46) L	11:13 PM	(2.07) H

TIDE TIMES

Tim Smith's

Brisbane Bar

Day	Date	Tide 1		
Sat	1	5:15 AM	(0.33)	L
Sun	2	5:59 AM	(0.42)	L
Mon	3	12:45 AM	(2.13)	H
Tue	4	1:35 AM	(2.13)	H
Wed	5	2:34 AM	(2.12)	H
THu	6	3:45 AM	(2.14)	H
Fri	7	5:05 AM	(2.19)	H
Sat	8	6:20 AM	(2.29)	H
Sun	9	12:36 AM	(0.62)	L
Mon	10	1:40 AM	(0.55)	L
Tue	11	2:32 AM	(0.48)	L
Wed	12 ○	3:16 AM	(0.44)	L
THu	13	3:54 AM	(0.43)	L
Fri	14	4:29 AM	(0.46)	L
Sat	15	5:01 AM	(0.51)	L
Sun	16	5:34 AM	(0.59)	L
Mon	17	12:05 AM	(2.06)	H
Tue	18	12:41 AM	(2.05)	H
Wed	19	1:21 AM	(2.01)	H
THu	20	2:10 AM	(1.96)	H
Fri	21	3:15 AM	(1.93)	H
Sat	22	4:39 AM	(1.96)	H
Sun	23	5:56 AM	(2.07)	H
Mon	24	12:00 AM	(0.76)	L
Tue	25	1:03 AM	(0.63)	L
Wed	26	1:59 AM	(0.50)	L
THu	27	2:48 AM	(0.39)	L
Fri	28 ●	3:35 AM	(0.32)	L

POPULAR TIDE ADJUSTMENTS

Ballina	-1hr 10min
Bribie Island	-10min
Brunswick Heads	-1hr 20min
Bundaberg	-55min
Burleigh Heads	-1hr 30 min
Byron Bay	-1hr 20min
Caloundra	-1hr 25min
Cleveland	+15min
Coomera River	+1hr 30min
Donnybrook	+1hr
Fraser Island East	-1hr 20min
Gladstone	-20min
Gold Coast Seaway	-1hr 15min
Hervey Bay	+1hr
Jumpinpin	-1hr 30min
Manly	+15min
Mooloolaba	-1hr 20min
Nerang River	+1hr
Noosa	-1hr 30min
Point Danger	-1hr 30min
Redcliffe	0
Redland Bay	+30min
Runaway Bay	-30min
Sanctuary Cove	+30min
Scarborough	+5min
Southport Broadwater	-35min
Tangalooma	-30min
Tin Can Bay	-45min
Toorbul	+30min
Tweed Heads	-45min
Urngan	-45min
Victoria Pt	+15min
Brunswick Heads	- 11hr 15min
Cabbage Tree Pt	+ 30min
Cape Moreton	- 1hr 15min
Jacobs Well	+ 14min
Peel Island	+12min
Rainbow Beach	- 1hr 20min
Tallebudgera Bridge	- 1hr 18min
Tewantin	- 15min

FEBRUARY 2025

Tide 2		Tide 3		Tide 4	
11:36 AM	(2.63) H	6:18 PM	(0.45) L	11:59 PM	(2.11) H
12:15 PM	(2.52) H	6:55 PM	(0.45) L		
6:46 AM	(0.54) L	12:54 PM	(2.36) H	7:31 PM	(0.48) L
7:39 AM	(0.70) L	1:38 PM	(2.15) H	8:13 PM	(0.53) L
8:44 AM	(0.85) L	2:30 PM	(1.92) H	9:02 PM	(0.59) L
10:08 AM	(0.95) L	3:41 PM	(1.72) H	10:06 PM	(0.65) L
11:46 AM	(0.94) L	5:10 PM	(1.62) H	11:21 PM	(0.66) L
1:12 PM	(0.83) L	6:35 PM	(1.64) H		
7:22 AM	(2.40) H	2:14 PM	(0.71) L	7:43 PM	(1.72) H
8:15 AM	(2.48) H	3:03 PM	(0.63) L	8:34 PM	(1.81) H
9:00 AM	(2.52) H	3:45 PM	(0.59) L	9:17 PM	(1.89) H
9:38 AM	(2.53) H	4:21 PM	(0.58) L	9:54 PM	(1.95) H
10:14 AM	(2.51) H	4:52 PM	(0.58) L	10:29 PM	(2.00) H
10:45 AM	(2.46) H	5:19 PM	(0.58) L	11:00 PM	(2.03) H
11:15 AM	(2.39) H	5:44 PM	(0.57) L	11:32 PM	(2.06) H
11:42 AM	(2.30) H	6:08 PM	(0.57) L		
6:08 AM	(0.69) L	12:10 PM	(2.17) H	6:34 PM	(0.59) L
6:45 AM	(0.81) L	12:40 PM	(2.02) H	7:03 PM	(0.64) L
7:30 AM	(0.93) L	1:14 PM	(1.85) H	7:37 PM	(0.72) L
8:25 AM	(1.04) L	1:59 PM	(1.68) H	8:20 PM	(0.80) L
9:44 AM	(1.10) L	3:05 PM	(1.56) H	9:24 PM	(0.86) L
11:23 AM	(1.07) L	4:37 PM	(1.52) H	10:45 PM	(0.85) L
12:43 PM	(0.95) L	6:00 PM	(1.59) H		
6:56 AM	(2.23) H	1:40 PM	(0.82) L	7:02 PM	(1.71) H
7:45 AM	(2.38) H	2:28 PM	(0.69) L	7:54 PM	(1.85) H
8:30 AM	(2.52) H	3:12 PM	(0.57) L	8:42 PM	(1.99) H
9:13 AM	(2.62) H	3:53 PM	(0.48) L	9:27 PM	(2.11) H
9:53 AM	(2.67) H	4:32 PM	(0.40) L	10:12 PM	(2.22) H

TIDE TIMES

Tim Smith's

POPULAR TIDE ADJUSTMENTS

Ballina	-1hr 10min
Bribie Island	-10min
Brunswick Heads	-1hr 20min
Bundaberg	-55min
Burleigh Heads	-1hr 30 min
Byron Bay	-1hr 20min
Caloundra	-1hr 25min
Cleveland	+15min
Coomera River	+1hr 30min
Donnybrook	+1hr
Fraser Island East	-1hr 20min
Gladstone	-20min
Gold Coast Seaway	-1hr 15min
Hervey Bay	+1hr
Jumpinpin	-1hr 30min
Manly	+15min
Mooloolaba	-1hr 20min
Nerang River	+1hr
Noosa	-1hr 30min
Point Danger	-1hr 30min
Redcliffe	0
Redland Bay	+30min
Runaway Bay	-30min
Sanctuary Cove	+30min
Scarborough	+5min
Southport Broadwater	-35min
Tangalooma	-30min
Tin Can Bay	-45min
Toorbul	+30min
Tweed Heads	-45min
Urngan	-45min
Victoria Pt	+15min
Brunswick Heads	- 11hr 15min
Cabbage Tree Pt	+ 30min
Cape Moreton	- 1hr 15min
Jacobs Well	+ 14min
Peel Island	+12min
Rainbow Beach	- 1hr 20min
Tallebudgera Bridge	- 1hr 18min
Tewantin	- 15min

Brisbane Bar

Day	Date	Tide 1	
Sat	1	4:20 AM	(0.30) L
Sun	2	5:06 AM	(0.34) L
Mon	3	5:51 AM	(0.43) L
Tue	4	12:25 AM	(2.37) H
Wed	5	1:14 AM	(2.34) H
THu	6	2:10 AM	(2.27) H
Fri	7	3:21 AM	(2.21) H
Sat	8	4:45 AM	(2.19) H
Sun	9	6:02 AM	(2.25) H
Mon	10	12:30 AM	(0.73) L
Tue	11	1:30 AM	(0.63) L
Wed	12	2:19 AM	(0.55) L
THu	13	3:00 AM	(0.51) L
Fri	14 ○	3:36 AM	(0.50) L
Sat	15	4:10 AM	(0.52) L
Sun	16	4:43 AM	(0.57) L
Mon	17	5:15 AM	(0.63) L
Tue	18	5:48 AM	(0.71) L
Wed	19	12:08 AM	(2.22) H
THu	20	12:44 AM	(2.16) H
Fri	21	1:25 AM	(2.09) H
Sat	22	2:21 AM	(2.03) H
Sun	23	3:42 AM	(2.01) H
Mon	24	5:07 AM	(2.09) H
Tue	25	6:14 AM	(2.23) H
Wed	26	12:35 AM	(0.68) L
THu	27	1:34 AM	(0.54) L
Fri	28	2:29 AM	(0.43) L
Sat	29 ●	3:19 AM	(0.37) L
Sun	30	4:08 AM	(0.35) L
Mon	31	4:56 AM	(0.39) L

Tide 2		Tide 3		Tide 4	
10:32 AM	(2.65) H	5:09 PM	(0.36) L	10:55 PM	(2.31) H
11:11 AM	(2.55) H	5:45 PM	(0.35) L	11:40 PM	(2.36) H
11:50 AM	(2.39) H	6:18 PM	(0.39) L		
6:40 AM	(0.58) L	12:30 PM	(2.17) H	6:53 PM	(0.46) L
7:34 AM	(0.74) L	1:15 PM	(1.93) H	7:32 PM	(0.57) L
8:43 AM	(0.89) L	2:13 PM	(1.71) H	8:23 PM	(0.68) L
10:15 AM	(0.96) L	3:40 PM	(1.55) H	9:36 PM	(0.78) L
11:51 AM	(0.90) L	5:20 PM	(1.56) H	11:08 PM	(0.80) L
1:02 PM	(0.79) L	6:38 PM	(1.67) H		
7:04 AM	(2.33) H	1:55 PM	(0.69) L	7:34 PM	(1.81) H
7:53 AM	(2.39) H	2:37 PM	(0.62) L	8:18 PM	(1.94) H
8:34 AM	(2.42) H	3:13 PM	(0.58) L	8:57 PM	(2.03) H
9:11 AM	(2.41) H	3:45 PM	(0.56) L	9:30 PM	(2.10) H
9:42 AM	(2.38) H	4:12 PM	(0.54) L	10:01 PM	(2.16) H
10:12 AM	(2.33) H	4:36 PM	(0.52) L	10:32 PM	(2.21) H
10:39 AM	(2.26) H	5:00 PM	(0.51) L	11:03 PM	(2.24) H
11:06 AM	(2.16) H	5:23 PM	(0.52) L	11:34 PM	(2.25) H
11:34 AM	(2.03) H	5:49 PM	(0.56) L		
6:24 AM	(0.81) L	12:04 PM	(1.89) H	6:16 PM	(0.63) L
7:04 AM	(0.91) L	12:38 PM	(1.75) H	6:46 PM	(0.72) L
7:55 AM	(1.00) L	1:22 PM	(1.62) H	7:27 PM	(0.81) L
9:08 AM	(1.06) L	2:30 PM	(1.52) H	8:29 PM	(0.89) L
10:44 AM	(1.02) L	4:08 PM	(1.52) H	10:00 PM	(0.91) L
12:03 PM	(0.91) L	5:34 PM	(1.63) H	11:25 PM	(0.82) L
1:02 PM	(0.76) L	6:38 PM	(1.80) H		
7:07 AM	(2.38) H	1:52 PM	(0.62) L	7:30 PM	(1.98) H
7:55 AM	(2.50) H	2:36 PM	(0.49) L	8:19 PM	(2.15) H
8:39 AM	(2.56) H	3:17 PM	(0.40) L	9:05 PM	(2.31) H
9:21 AM	(2.56) H	3:56 PM	(0.33) L	9:50 PM	(2.44) H
10:02 AM	(2.48) H	4:32 PM	(0.30) L	10:34 PM	(2.54) H
10:45 AM	(2.34) H	5:08 PM	(0.31) L	11:19 PM	(2.58) H

TIDE TIMES

Tim Smith's

POPULAR TIDE ADJUSTMENTS

Ballina	-1hr 10min
Bribie Island	-10min
Brunswick Heads	-1hr 20min
Bundaberg	-55min
Burleigh Heads	-1hr 30 min
Byron Bay	-1hr 20min
Caloundra	-1hr 25min
Cleveland	+15min
Coomera River	+1hr 30min
Donnybrook	+1hr
Fraser Island East	-1hr 20min
Gladstone	-20min
Gold Coast Seaway	-1hr 15min
Hervey Bay	+1hr
Jumpinpin	-1hr 30min
Manly	+15min
Mooloolaba	-1hr 20min
Nerang River	+1hr
Noosa	-1hr 30min
Point Danger	-1hr 30min
Redcliffe	0
Redland Bay	+30min
Runaway Bay	-30min
Sanctuary Cove	+30min
Scarborough	+5min
Southport Broadwater	-35min
Tangalooma	-30min
Tin Can Bay	-45min
Toorbul	+30min
Tweed Heads	-45min
Urngan	-45min
Victoria Pt	+15min
Brunswick Heads	- 11hr 15min
Cabbage Tree Pt	+ 30min
Cape Moreton	- 1hr 15min
Jacobs Well	+ 14min
Peel Island	+12min
Rainbow Beach	- 1hr 20min
Tallebudgera Bridge	- 1hr 18min
Tewantin	- 15min

Brisbane Bar

Day	Date	Tide 1	
Tue	1	5:45 AM	(0.49) L
Wed	2	12:05 AM	(2.56) H
THu	3	12:55 AM	(2.48) H
Fri	4	1:51 AM	(2.37) H
Sat	5	3:00 AM	(2.25) H
Sun	6	4:18 AM	(2.19) H
Mon	7	5:32 AM	(2.20) H
Tue	8	12:10 AM	(0.81) L
Wed	9	1:08 AM	(0.72) L
THu	10	1:55 AM	(0.65) L
Fri	11	2:36 AM	(0.62) L
Sat	12	3:14 AM	(0.60) L
Sun	13 ○	3:50 AM	(0.61) L
Mon	14	4:25 AM	(0.63) L
Tue	15	4:59 AM	(0.67) L
Wed	16	5:32 AM	(0.73) L
THu	17	6:08 AM	(0.80) L
Fri	18	12:15 AM	(2.27) H
Sat	19	12:57 AM	(2.21) H
Sun	20	1:50 AM	(2.15) H
Mon	21	3:00 AM	(2.13) H
Tue	22	4:17 AM	(2.17) H
Wed	23	5:26 AM	(2.27) H
THu	24	12:03 AM	(0.71) L
Fri	25	1:08 AM	(0.60) L
Sat	26	2:07 AM	(0.52) L
Sun	27	3:02 AM	(0.46) L
Mon	28 ●	3:56 AM	(0.44) L
Tue	29	4:47 AM	(0.47) L
Wed	30	5:41 AM	(0.53) L

Tide 2	Tide 3	Tide 4
11:27 AM (2.15) H	5:43 PM (0.38) L	
6:36 AM (0.62) L	12:12 PM (1.94) H	6:19 PM (0.48) L
7:36 AM (0.75) L	1:04 PM (1.73) H	7:00 PM (0.62) L
8:49 AM (0.86) L	2:13 PM (1.58) H	7:56 PM (0.77) L
10:14 AM (0.89) L	3:46 PM (1.53) H	9:17 PM (0.87) L
11:30 AM (0.84) L	5:14 PM (1.61) H	10:53 PM (0.88) L
12:30 PM (0.76) L	6:19 PM (1.76) H	
6:31 AM (2.24) H	1:18 PM (0.68) L	7:10 PM (1.92) H
7:18 AM (2.27) H	1:57 PM (0.61) L	7:51 PM (2.05) H
7:59 AM (2.27) H	2:30 PM (0.57) L	8:28 PM (2.15) H
8:33 AM (2.25) H	3:00 PM (0.53) L	9:01 PM (2.24) H
9:05 AM (2.21) H	3:27 PM (0.50) L	9:33 PM (2.30) H
9:35 AM (2.15) H	3:52 PM (0.48) L	10:05 PM (2.36) H
10:04 AM (2.08) H	4:17 PM (0.48) L	10:36 PM (2.38) H
10:33 AM (1.99) H	4:44 PM (0.51) L	11:08 PM (2.37) H
11:04 AM (1.88) H	5:12 PM (0.56) L	11:41 PM (2.33) H
11:38 AM (1.78) H	5:41 PM (0.63) L	
6:48 AM (0.88) L	12:15 PM (1.68) H	6:14 PM (0.71) L
7:39 AM (0.94) L	1:04 PM (1.60) H	6:58 PM (0.80) L
8:47 AM (0.96) L	2:14 PM (1.56) H	8:00 PM (0.87) L
10:07 AM (0.92) L	3:45 PM (1.60) H	9:26 PM (0.88) L
11:17 AM (0.81) L	5:04 PM (1.73) H	10:50 PM (0.82) L
12:16 PM (0.67) L	6:08 PM (1.92) H	
6:23 AM (2.36) H	1:08 PM (0.54) L	7:03 PM (2.12) H
7:15 AM (2.41) H	1:55 PM (0.43) L	7:53 PM (2.31) H
8:02 AM (2.40) H	2:37 PM (0.34) L	8:41 PM (2.48) H
8:48 AM (2.34) H	3:17 PM (0.29) L	9:28 PM (2.62) H
9:35 AM (2.23) H	3:56 PM (0.28) L	10:15 PM (2.70) H
10:22 AM (2.09) H	4:34 PM (0.32) L	11:01 PM (2.72) H
11:11 AM (1.93) H	5:13 PM (0.40) L	11:49 PM (2.66) H

TIDE TIMES

Tim Smith's

Brisbane Bar

POPULAR TIDE ADJUSTMENTS

Ballina	-1hr 10min
Bribie Island	-10min
Brunswick Heads	-1hr 20min
Bundaberg	-55min
Burleigh Heads	-1hr 30 min
Byron Bay	-1hr 20min
Caloundra	-1hr 25min
Cleveland	+15min
Coomera River	+1hr 30min
Donnybrook	+1hr
Fraser Island East	-1hr 20min
Gladstone	-20min
Gold Coast Seaway	-1hr 15min
Hervey Bay	+1hr
Jumpinpin	-1hr 30min
Manly	+15min
Mooloolaba	-1hr 20min
Nerang River	+1hr
Noosa	-1hr 30min
Point Danger	-1hr 30min
Redcliffe	0
Redland Bay	+30min
Runaway Bay	-30min
Sanctuary Cove	+30min
Scarborough	+5min
Southport Broadwater	-35min
Tangalooma	-30min
Tin Can Bay	-45min
Toorbul	+30min
Tweed Heads	-45min
Urngan	-45min
Victoria Pt	+15min
Brunswick Heads	- 11hr 15min
Cabbage Tree Pt	+ 30min
Cape Moreton	- 1hr 15min
Jacobs Well	+ 14min
Peel Island	+12min
Rainbow Beach	- 1hr 20min
Tallebudgera Bridge	- 1hr 18min
Tewantin	- 15min

Day	Date		Tide 1	
THu	1		6:36 AM	(0.63) L
Fri	2		12:39 AM	(2.55) H
Sat	3		1:33 AM	(2.42) H
Sun	4		2:33 AM	(2.28) H
Mon	5		3:40 AM	(2.19) H
Tue	6		4:45 AM	(2.14) H
Wed	7		5:43 AM	(2.12) H
THu	8		12:33 AM	(0.83) L
Fri	9		1:24 AM	(0.78) L
Sat	10		2:09 AM	(0.73) L
Sun	11		2:50 AM	(0.70) L
Mon	12		3:30 AM	(0.68) L
Tue	13	◯	4:08 AM	(0.68) L
Wed	14		4:45 AM	(0.70) L
THu	15		5:21 AM	(0.74) L
Fri	16		5:59 AM	(0.78) L
Sat	17		6:41 AM	(0.82) L
Sun	18		12:41 AM	(2.31) H
Mon	19		1:31 AM	(2.28) H
Tue	20		2:30 AM	(2.25) H
Wed	21		3:35 AM	(2.25) H
THu	22		4:39 AM	(2.26) H
Fri	23		5:39 AM	(2.26) H
Sat	24		12:44 AM	(0.68) L
Sun	25		1:50 AM	(0.61) L
Mon	26		2:51 AM	(0.56) L
Tue	27	●	3:48 AM	(0.52) L
Wed	28		4:44 AM	(0.52) L
THu	29		5:38 AM	(0.55) L
Fri	30		6:31 AM	(0.60) L
Sat	31		12:22 AM	(2.56) H

Tide 2		Tide 3		Tide 4	
12:02 PM	(1.78) H	5:54 PM	(0.52) L		
7:37 AM	(0.72) L	1:00 PM	(1.65) H	6:41 PM	(0.66) L
8:43 AM	(0.79) L	2:09 PM	(1.59) H	7:39 PM	(0.80) L
9:47 AM	(0.81) L	3:28 PM	(1.60) H	8:56 PM	(0.90) L
10:48 AM	(0.79) L	4:43 PM	(1.69) H	10:20 PM	(0.92) L
11:41 AM	(0.74) L	5:44 PM	(1.83) H	11:33 PM	(0.89) L
12:27 PM	(0.67) L	6:34 PM	(1.98) H		
6:31 AM	(2.11) H	1:06 PM	(0.61) L	7:17 PM	(2.11) H
7:14 AM	(2.10) H	1:41 PM	(0.55) L	7:56 PM	(2.23) H
7:51 AM	(2.06) H	2:13 PM	(0.51) L	8:31 PM	(2.33) H
8:27 AM	(2.02) H	2:43 PM	(0.48) L	9:06 PM	(2.40) H
9:00 AM	(1.96) H	3:12 PM	(0.47) L	9:39 PM	(2.44) H
9:34 AM	(1.91) H	3:42 PM	(0.48) L	10:13 PM	(2.45) H
10:08 AM	(1.85) H	4:12 PM	(0.51) L	10:46 PM	(2.44) H
10:44 AM	(1.79) H	4:44 PM	(0.55) L	11:21 PM	(2.40) H
11:22 AM	(1.74) H	5:17 PM	(0.60) L	11:59 PM	(2.36) H
12:05 PM	(1.69) H	5:56 PM	(0.66) L		
7:30 AM	(0.84) L	12:58 PM	(1.66) H	6:44 PM	(0.73) L
8:30 AM	(0.83) L	2:02 PM	(1.66) H	7:45 PM	(0.79) L
9:32 AM	(0.78) L	3:18 PM	(1.72) H	9:00 PM	(0.82) L
10:32 AM	(0.68) L	4:32 PM	(1.85) H	10:18 PM	(0.80) L
11:29 AM	(0.57) L	5:37 PM	(2.03) H	11:32 PM	(0.75) L
12:21 PM	(0.47) L	6:35 PM	(2.23) H		
6:35 AM	(2.22) H	1:11 PM	(0.39) L	7:29 PM	(2.42) H
7:29 AM	(2.16) H	1:58 PM	(0.33) L	8:20 PM	(2.58) H
8:22 AM	(2.07) H	2:43 PM	(0.31) L	9:10 PM	(2.70) H
9:15 AM	(1.98) H	3:26 PM	(0.31) L	9:59 PM	(2.75) H
10:08 AM	(1.89) H	4:09 PM	(0.35) L	10:46 PM	(2.74) H
11:00 AM	(1.80) H	4:53 PM	(0.42) L	11:34 PM	(2.68) H
11:54 AM	(1.74) H	5:38 PM	(0.52) L		
7:24 AM	(0.67) L	12:48 PM	(1.69) H	6:26 PM	(0.64) L

TIDE TIMES

Tim Smith's

Brisbane Bar

POPULAR TIDE ADJUSTMENTS

Ballina	-1hr 10min
Bribie Island	-10min
Brunswick Heads	-1hr 20min
Bundaberg	-55min
Burleigh Heads	-1hr 30 min
Byron Bay	-1hr 20min
Caloundra	-1hr 25min
Cleveland	+15min
Coomera River	+1hr 30min
Donnybrook	+1hr
Fraser Island East	-1hr 20min
Gladstone	-20min
Gold Coast Seaway	-1hr 15min
Hervey Bay	+1hr
Jumpinpin	-1hr 30min
Manly	+15min
Mooloolaba	-1hr 20min
Nerang River	+1hr
Noosa	-1hr 30min
Point Danger	-1hr 30min
Redcliffe	0
Redland Bay	+30min
Runaway Bay	-30min
Sanctuary Cove	+30min
Scarborough	+5min
Southport Broadwater	-35min
Tangalooma	-30min
Tin Can Bay	-45min
Toorbul	+30min
Tweed Heads	-45min
Urngan	-45min
Victoria Pt	+15min
Brunswick Heads	- 11hr 15min
Cabbage Tree Pt	+ 30min
Cape Moreton	- 1hr 15min
Jacobs Well	+ 14min
Peel Island	+12min
Rainbow Beach	- 1hr 20min
Tallebudgera Bridge	- 1hr 18min
Tewantin	- 15min

Day	Date	Tide 1		
Sun	1	1:10 AM	(2.43)	H
Mon	2	1:59 AM	(2.29)	H
Tue	3	2:51 AM	(2.17)	H
Wed	4	3:45 AM	(2.07)	H
THu	5	4:41 AM	(1.99)	H
Fri	6	5:34 AM	(1.94)	H
Sat	7	12:50 AM	(0.89)	L
Sun	8	1:43 AM	(0.82)	L
Mon	9	2:30 AM	(0.76)	L
Tue	10	3:13 AM	(0.72)	L
Wed	11 ◯	3:53 AM	(0.69)	L
THu	12	4:33 AM	(0.69)	L
Fri	13	5:13 AM	(0.70)	L
Sat	14	5:52 AM	(0.71)	L
Sun	15	6:34 AM	(0.71)	L
Mon	16	12:27 AM	(2.42)	H
Tue	17	1:12 AM	(2.38)	H
Wed	18	2:00 AM	(2.32)	H
THu	19	2:56 AM	(2.24)	H
Fri	20	3:57 AM	(2.15)	H
Sat	21	5:01 AM	(2.05)	H
Sun	22	12:29 AM	(0.77)	L
Mon	23	1:43 AM	(0.69)	L
Tue	24	2:47 AM	(0.61)	L
Wed	25 ●	3:45 AM	(0.55)	L
THu	26	4:39 AM	(0.52)	L
Fri	27	5:28 AM	(0.53)	L
Sat	28	6:13 AM	(0.57)	L
Sun	29	12:00 AM	(2.53)	H
Mon	30	12:39 AM	(2.41)	H

Tide 2		Tide 3		Tide 4	
8:15 AM	(0.72) L	1:45 PM	(1.67) H	7:19 PM	(0.77) L
9:04 AM	(0.74) L	2:47 PM	(1.69) H	8:21 PM	(0.88) L
9:52 AM	(0.74) L	3:54 PM	(1.75) H	9:31 PM	(0.95) L
10:39 AM	(0.71) L	4:57 PM	(1.85) H	10:44 PM	(0.97) L
11:24 AM	(0.66) L	5:52 PM	(1.98) H	11:51 PM	(0.94) L
12:07 PM	(0.61) L	6:40 PM	(2.12) H		
6:24 AM	(1.90) H	12:47 PM	(0.56) L	7:23 PM	(2.24) H
7:09 AM	(1.86) H	1:27 PM	(0.52) L	8:02 PM	(2.35) H
7:52 AM	(1.83) H	2:03 PM	(0.49) L	8:41 PM	(2.42) H
8:31 AM	(1.81) H	2:39 PM	(0.48) L	9:17 PM	(2.46) H
9:11 AM	(1.79) H	3:15 PM	(0.48) L	9:54 PM	(2.47) H
9:50 AM	(1.78) H	3:50 PM	(0.48) L	10:30 PM	(2.47) H
10:30 AM	(1.77) H	4:27 PM	(0.50) L	11:08 PM	(2.46) H
11:13 AM	(1.77) H	5:05 PM	(0.53) L	11:46 PM	(2.45) H
11:59 AM	(1.76) H	5:47 PM	(0.57) L		
7:18 AM	(0.70) L	12:49 PM	(1.77) H	6:36 PM	(0.63) L
8:06 AM	(0.68) L	1:46 PM	(1.79) H	7:32 PM	(0.71) L
8:57 AM	(0.63) L	2:51 PM	(1.85) H	8:37 PM	(0.77) L
9:48 AM	(0.57) L	4:00 PM	(1.96) H	9:51 PM	(0.81) L
10:43 AM	(0.51) L	5:08 PM	(2.11) H	11:10 PM	(0.81) L
11:38 AM	(0.45) L	6:12 PM	(2.29) H		
6:05 AM	(1.96) H	12:33 PM	(0.40) L	7:10 PM	(2.46) H
7:07 AM	(1.89) H	1:27 PM	(0.37) L	8:05 PM	(2.59) H
8:09 AM	(1.84) H	2:19 PM	(0.35) L	8:58 PM	(2.68) H
9:07 AM	(1.81) H	3:08 PM	(0.34) L	9:46 PM	(2.72) H
10:00 AM	(1.80) H	3:56 PM	(0.36) L	10:33 PM	(2.70) H
10:51 AM	(1.79) H	4:41 PM	(0.41) L	11:17 PM	(2.63) H
11:38 AM	(1.79) H	5:25 PM	(0.49) L		
6:54 AM	(0.61) L	12:24 PM	(1.78) H	6:08 PM	(0.59) L
7:32 AM	(0.65) L	1:09 PM	(1.77) H	6:52 PM	(0.71) L

TIDE TIMES

Tim Smith's

POPULAR TIDE ADJUSTMENTS

Ballina	-1hr 10min
Bribie Island	-10min
Brunswick Heads	-1hr 20min
Bundaberg	-55min
Burleigh Heads	-1hr 30 min
Byron Bay	-1hr 20min
Caloundra	-1hr 25min
Cleveland	+15min
Coomera River	+1hr 30min
Donnybrook	+1hr
Fraser Island East	-1hr 20min
Gladstone	-20min
Gold Coast Seaway	-1hr 15min
Hervey Bay	+1hr
Jumpinpin	-1hr 30min
Manly	+15min
Mooloolaba	-1hr 20min
Nerang River	+1hr
Noosa	-1hr 30min
Point Danger	-1hr 30min
Redcliffe	0
Redland Bay	+30min
Runaway Bay	-30min
Sanctuary Cove	+30min
Scarborough	+5min
Southport Broadwater	-35min
Tangalooma	-30min
Tin Can Bay	-45min
Toorbul	+30min
Tweed Heads	-45min
Urngan	-45min
Victoria Pt	+15min
Brunswick Heads	- 11hr 15min
Cabbage Tree Pt	+ 30min
Cape Moreton	- 1hr 15min
Jacobs Well	+ 14min
Peel Island	+12min
Rainbow Beach	- 1hr 20min
Tallebudgera Bridge	- 1hr 18min
Tewantin	- 15min

Brisbane Bar

Day	Date	Tide 1		
Tue	1	1:18 AM	(2.27)	H
Wed	2	1:58 AM	(2.12)	H
THu	3	2:42 AM	(1.98)	H
Fri	4	3:34 AM	(1.85)	H
Sat	5	4:35 AM	(1.75)	H
Sun	6	12:19 AM	(0.96)	L
Mon	7	1:20 AM	(0.87)	L
Tue	8	2:11 AM	(0.78)	L
Wed	9	2:57 AM	(0.71)	L
THu	10	3:39 AM	(0.66)	L
Fri	11 ○	4:19 AM	(0.63)	L
Sat	12	4:59 AM	(0.60)	L
Sun	13	5:38 AM	(0.58)	L
Mon	14	6:17 AM	(0.56)	L
Tue	15	12:08 AM	(2.48)	H
Wed	16	12:47 AM	(2.39)	H
THu	17	1:30 AM	(2.26)	H
Fri	18	2:20 AM	(2.10)	H
Sat	19	3:22 AM	(1.92)	H
Sun	20	4:36 AM	(1.78)	H
Mon	21	12:30 AM	(0.81)	L
Tue	22	1:46 AM	(0.69)	L
Wed	23	2:47 AM	(0.59)	L
THu	24	3:40 AM	(0.52)	L
Fri	25 ●	4:25 AM	(0.49)	L
Sat	26	5:05 AM	(0.49)	L
Sun	27	5:41 AM	(0.51)	L
Mon	28	6:13 AM	(0.54)	L
Tue	29	12:03 AM	(2.34)	H
Wed	30	12:34 AM	(2.20)	H
THu	31	1:07 AM	(2.04)	H

Tide 2		Tide 3		Tide 4	
8:09 AM	(0.67) L	1:58 PM	(1.78) **H**	7:41 PM	(0.83) L
8:47 AM	(0.68) L	2:53 PM	(1.80) **H**	8:39 PM	(0.95) L
9:30 AM	(0.67) L	3:57 PM	(1.85) **H**	9:48 PM	(1.02) L
10:16 AM	(0.66) L	5:02 PM	(1.94) **H**	11:06 PM	(1.02) L
11:07 AM	(0.64) L	6:00 PM	(2.06) **H**		
5:37 AM	(1.69) **H**	11:58 AM	(0.61) L	6:51 PM	(2.19) **H**
6:35 AM	(1.68) **H**	12:46 PM	(0.57) L	7:36 PM	(2.29) **H**
7:26 AM	(1.69) **H**	1:32 PM	(0.52) L	8:18 PM	(2.38) **H**
8:12 AM	(1.72) **H**	2:15 PM	(0.48) L	8:59 PM	(2.44) **H**
8:55 AM	(1.75) **H**	2:56 PM	(0.44) L	9:37 PM	(2.48) **H**
9:37 AM	(1.79) **H**	3:36 PM	(0.42) L	10:15 PM	(2.52) **H**
10:19 AM	(1.83) **H**	4:17 PM	(0.40) L	10:53 PM	(2.53) **H**
11:03 AM	(1.86) **H**	4:59 PM	(0.42) L	11:30 PM	(2.53) **H**
11:48 AM	(1.89) **H**	5:42 PM	(0.47) L		
6:56 AM	(0.54) L	12:35 PM	(1.91) **H**	6:28 PM	(0.55) L
7:35 AM	(0.52) L	1:27 PM	(1.94) **H**	7:19 PM	(0.65) L
8:17 AM	(0.51) L	2:24 PM	(1.98) **H**	8:19 PM	(0.77) L
9:05 AM	(0.51) L	3:30 PM	(2.05) **H**	9:33 PM	(0.85) L
10:01 AM	(0.51) L	4:44 PM	(2.15) **H**	11:00 PM	(0.87) L
11:03 AM	(0.50) L	5:55 PM	(2.28) **H**		
5:53 AM	(1.70) **H**	12:08 PM	(0.47) L	7:00 PM	(2.42) **H**
7:06 AM	(1.70) **H**	1:12 PM	(0.43) L	7:58 PM	(2.54) **H**
8:10 AM	(1.73) **H**	2:10 PM	(0.39) L	8:48 PM	(2.61) **H**
9:04 AM	(1.78) **H**	3:01 PM	(0.35) L	9:35 PM	(2.64) **H**
9:52 AM	(1.82) **H**	3:48 PM	(0.35) L	10:16 PM	(2.61) **H**
10:34 AM	(1.86) **H**	4:30 PM	(0.38) L	10:55 PM	(2.55) **H**
11:15 AM	(1.88) **H**	5:09 PM	(0.45) L	11:30 PM	(2.46) **H**
11:53 AM	(1.89) **H**	5:46 PM	(0.55) L		
6:42 AM	(0.55) L	12:30 PM	(1.89) **H**	6:24 PM	(0.66) L
7:11 AM	(0.57) L	1:11 PM	(1.89) **H**	7:05 PM	(0.80) L
7:42 AM	(0.60) L	1:57 PM	(1.88) **H**	7:54 PM	(0.92) L

TIDE TIMES

Tam Smith's

POPULAR TIDE ADJUSTMENTS

Ballina	-1hr 10min
Bribie Island	-10min
Brunswick Heads	-1hr 20min
Bundaberg	-55min
Burleigh Heads	-1hr 30 min
Byron Bay	-1hr 20min
Caloundra	-1hr 25min
Cleveland	+15min
Coomera River	+1hr 30min
Donnybrook	+1hr
Fraser Island East	-1hr 20min
Gladstone	-20min
Gold Coast Seaway	-1hr 15min
Hervey Bay	+1hr
Jumpinpin	-1hr 30min
Manly	+15min
Mooloolaba	-1hr 20min
Nerang River	+1hr
Noosa	-1hr 30min
Point Danger	-1hr 30min
Redcliffe	0
Redland Bay	+30min
Runaway Bay	-30min
Sanctuary Cove	+30min
Scarborough	+5min
Southport Broadwater	-35min
Tangalooma	-30min
Tin Can Bay	-45min
Toorbul	+30min
Tweed Heads	-45min
Urngan	-45min
Victoria Pt	+15min
Brunswick Heads	- 11hr 15min
Cabbage Tree Pt	+ 30min
Cape Moreton	- 1hr 15min
Jacobs Well	+ 14min
Peel Island	+12min
Rainbow Beach	- 1hr 20min
Tallebudgera Bridge	- 1hr 18min
Tewantin	- 15min

Brisbane Bar

Day	Date		Tide 1	
Fri	1	1:44 AM	(1.86)	H
Sat	2	2:32 AM	(1.69)	H
Sun	3	3:39 AM	(1.56)	H
Mon	4	4:59 AM	(1.51)	H
Tue	5	1:00 AM	(0.88)	L
Wed	6	1:52 AM	(0.77)	L
THu	7	2:36 AM	(0.67)	L
Fri	8	3:17 AM	(0.59)	L
Sat	9	3:57 AM	(0.52)	L
Sun	10	4:35 AM	(0.46)	L
Mon	11	5:13 AM	(0.42)	L
Tue	12	5:49 AM	(0.39)	L
Wed	13	6:24 AM	(0.39)	L
THu	14	12:22 AM	(2.28)	H
Fri	15	1:03 AM	(2.08)	H
Sat	16	1:53 AM	(1.86)	H
Sun	17	3:01 AM	(1.66)	H
Mon	18	4:32 AM	(1.54)	H
Tue	19	12:40 AM	(0.77)	L
Wed	20	1:46 AM	(0.63)	L
THu	21	2:38 AM	(0.52)	L
Fri	22	3:21 AM	(0.46)	L
Sat	23 ●	4:00 AM	(0.44)	L
Sun	24	4:32 AM	(0.44)	L
Mon	25	5:00 AM	(0.44)	L
Tue	26	5:27 AM	(0.45)	L
Wed	27	5:51 AM	(0.45)	L
THu	28	6:16 AM	(0.48)	L
Fri	29	12:21 AM	(1.90)	H
Sat	30	12:55 AM	(1.73)	H
Sun	31	1:39 AM	(1.56)	H

Tide 2		Tide 3		Tide 4	
8:19 AM	(0.63) L	2:52 PM	(1.87) H	8:56 PM	(1.03) L
9:06 AM	(0.68) L	4:01 PM	(1.90) H	10:20 PM	(1.06) L
10:06 AM	(0.71) L	5:16 PM	(1.97) H	11:52 PM	(1.00) L
11:11 AM	(0.69) L	6:18 PM	(2.09) H		
6:10 AM	(1.54) H	12:12 PM	(0.64) L	7:10 PM	(2.21) H
7:07 AM	(1.61) H	1:06 PM	(0.55) L	7:55 PM	(2.32) H
7:55 AM	(1.70) H	1:56 PM	(0.47) L	8:37 PM	(2.42) H
8:39 AM	(1.79) H	2:41 PM	(0.39) L	9:16 PM	(2.50) H
9:22 AM	(1.87) H	3:25 PM	(0.34) L	9:54 PM	(2.56) H
10:05 AM	(1.95) H	4:08 PM	(0.31) L	10:31 PM	(2.57) H
10:48 AM	(2.01) H	4:50 PM	(0.34) L	11:07 PM	(2.54) H
11:32 AM	(2.06) H	5:34 PM	(0.40) L	11:44 PM	(2.44) H
12:17 PM	(2.09) H	6:19 PM	(0.51) L		
6:59 AM	(0.41) L	1:05 PM	(2.10) H	7:10 PM	(0.65) L
7:38 AM	(0.45) L	2:00 PM	(2.11) H	8:10 PM	(0.79) L
8:25 AM	(0.51) L	3:07 PM	(2.11) H	9:30 PM	(0.89) L
9:26 AM	(0.56) L	4:25 PM	(2.15) H	11:09 PM	(0.88) L
10:41 AM	(0.59) L	5:44 PM	(2.25) H		
6:02 AM	(1.56) H	11:59 AM	(0.55) L	6:51 PM	(2.36) H
7:14 AM	(1.66) H	1:09 PM	(0.47) L	7:47 PM	(2.46) H
8:09 AM	(1.76) H	2:06 PM	(0.40) L	8:35 PM	(2.52) H
8:55 AM	(1.85) H	2:55 PM	(0.35) L	9:16 PM	(2.52) H
9:35 AM	(1.92) H	3:37 PM	(0.35) L	9:53 PM	(2.49) H
10:12 AM	(1.97) H	4:15 PM	(0.39) L	10:26 PM	(2.43) H
10:46 AM	(2.00) H	4:50 PM	(0.45) L	10:56 PM	(2.33) H
11:20 AM	(2.02) H	5:24 PM	(0.54) L	11:24 PM	(2.21) H
11:54 AM	(2.03) H	5:59 PM	(0.65) L	11:52 PM	(2.07) H
12:30 PM	(2.02) H	6:36 PM	(0.77) L		
6:45 AM	(0.53) L	1:10 PM	(1.98) H	7:19 PM	(0.89) L
7:18 AM	(0.61) L	1:57 PM	(1.93) H	8:14 PM	(0.99) L
8:01 AM	(0.70) L	3:00 PM	(1.89) H	9:36 PM	(1.04) L

TIDE TIMES

Tim Smith's

Brisbane Bar

POPULAR TIDE ADJUSTMENTS

Ballina	-1hr 10min
Bribie Island	-10min
Brunswick Heads	-1hr 20min
Bundaberg	-55min
Burleigh Heads	-1hr 30 min
Byron Bay	-1hr 20min
Caloundra	-1hr 25min
Cleveland	+15min
Coomera River	+1hr 30min
Donnybrook	+1hr
Fraser Island East	-1hr 20min
Gladstone	-20min
Gold Coast Seaway	-1hr 15min
Hervey Bay	+1hr
Jumpinpin	-1hr 30min
Manly	+15min
Mooloolaba	-1hr 20min
Nerang River	+1hr
Noosa	-1hr 30min
Point Danger	-1hr 30min
Redcliffe	0
Redland Bay	+30min
Runaway Bay	-30min
Sanctuary Cove	+30min
Scarborough	+5min
Southport Broadwater	-35min
Tangalooma	-30min
Tin Can Bay	-45min
Toorbul	+30min
Tweed Heads	-45min
Urngan	-45min
Victoria Pt	+15min
Brunswick Heads	- 11hr 15min
Cabbage Tree Pt	+ 30min
Cape Moreton	- 1hr 15min
Jacobs Well	+ 14min
Peel Island	+12min
Rainbow Beach	- 1hr 20min
Tallebudgera Bridge	- 1hr 18min
Tewantin	- 15min

Day	Date		Tide 1	
Mon	1		2:47 AM	(1.43) **H**
Tue	2		4:25 AM	(1.40) **H**
Wed	3		12:33 AM	(0.87) L
THu	4		1:23 AM	(0.73) L
Fri	5		2:07 AM	(0.60) L
Sat	6		2:47 AM	(0.49) L
Sun	7		3:26 AM	(0.40) L
Mon	8	◯	4:03 AM	(0.32) L
Tue	9		4:40 AM	(0.27) L
Wed	10		5:15 AM	(0.26) L
THu	11		5:48 AM	(0.29) L
Fri	12		6:23 AM	(0.35) L
Sat	13		12:43 AM	(1.84) **H**
Sun	14		1:39 AM	(1.62) **H**
Mon	15		3:04 AM	(1.46) **H**
Tue	16		4:48 AM	(1.46) **H**
Wed	17		12:33 AM	(0.68) L
THu	18		1:29 AM	(0.56) L
Fri	19		2:13 AM	(0.47) L
Sat	20		2:50 AM	(0.42) L
Sun	21		3:23 AM	(0.40) L
Mon	22	●	3:51 AM	(0.39) L
Tue	23		4:16 AM	(0.37) L
Wed	24		4:41 AM	(0.37) L
THu	25		5:04 AM	(0.39) L
Fri	26		5:30 AM	(0.43) L
Sat	27		5:59 AM	(0.51) L
Sun	28		12:20 AM	(1.62) **H**
Mon	29		1:03 AM	(1.49) **H**
Tue	30		2:10 AM	(1.39) **H**

SEPTEMBER 2025

Tide 2		Tide 3		Tide 4	
9:03 AM	(0.77) L	4:22 PM	(1.90) H	11:21 PM	(0.99) L
10:24 AM	(0.78) L	5:39 PM	(2.00) H		
5:48 AM	(1.48) H	11:39 AM	(0.70) L	6:36 PM	(2.14) H
6:46 AM	(1.62) H	12:41 PM	(0.58) L	7:24 PM	(2.28) H
7:34 AM	(1.76) H	1:34 PM	(0.46) L	8:07 PM	(2.41) H
8:18 AM	(1.89) H	2:23 PM	(0.36) L	8:47 PM	(2.49) H
9:02 AM	(2.01) H	3:10 PM	(0.30) L	9:26 PM	(2.53) H
9:45 AM	(2.12) H	3:55 PM	(0.28) L	10:03 PM	(2.51) H
10:29 AM	(2.21) H	4:41 PM	(0.31) L	10:41 PM	(2.43) H
11:13 AM	(2.27) H	5:26 PM	(0.39) L	11:18 PM	(2.27) H
11:58 AM	(2.29) H	6:14 PM	(0.52) L	11:59 PM	(2.07) H
12:46 PM	(2.27) H	7:07 PM	(0.66) L		
7:01 AM	(0.44) L	1:41 PM	(2.22) H	8:13 PM	(0.79) L
7:52 AM	(0.56) L	2:49 PM	(2.17) H	9:43 PM	(0.86) L
9:03 AM	(0.65) L	4:10 PM	(2.15) H	11:19 PM	(0.81) L
10:32 AM	(0.67) L	5:30 PM	(2.21) H		
6:08 AM	(1.58) H	11:55 AM	(0.61) L	6:35 PM	(2.29) H
7:07 AM	(1.74) H	1:01 PM	(0.51) L	7:28 PM	(2.36) H
7:55 AM	(1.87) H	1:54 PM	(0.44) L	8:11 PM	(2.39) H
8:35 AM	(1.97) H	2:39 PM	(0.40) L	8:48 PM	(2.37) H
9:11 AM	(2.05) H	3:18 PM	(0.41) L	9:21 PM	(2.32) H
9:45 AM	(2.11) H	3:55 PM	(0.44) L	9:52 PM	(2.25) H
10:17 AM	(2.15) H	4:30 PM	(0.50) L	10:20 PM	(2.16) H
10:49 AM	(2.17) H	5:03 PM	(0.57) L	10:47 PM	(2.04) H
11:22 AM	(2.17) H	5:37 PM	(0.65) L	11:16 PM	(1.91) H
11:56 AM	(2.14) H	6:13 PM	(0.74) L	11:46 PM	(1.77) H
12:32 PM	(2.08) H	6:53 PM	(0.84) L		
6:30 AM	(0.61) L	1:15 PM	(2.01) H	7:44 PM	(0.93) L
7:11 AM	(0.71) L	2:10 PM	(1.94) H	8:57 PM	(0.99) L
8:12 AM	(0.80) L	3:25 PM	(1.92) H	10:35 PM	(0.95) L

TIDE TIMES

Tim Smith's

Brisbane Bar

POPULAR TIDE ADJUSTMENTS

Ballina	-1hr 10min
Bribie Island	-10min
Brunswick Heads	-1hr 20min
Bundaberg	-55min
Burleigh Heads	-1hr 30 min
Byron Bay	-1hr 20min
Caloundra	-1hr 25min
Cleveland	+15min
Coomera River	+1hr 30min
Donnybrook	+1hr
Fraser Island East	-1hr 20min
Gladstone	-20min
Gold Coast Seaway	-1hr 15min
Hervey Bay	+1hr
Jumpinpin	-1hr 30min
Manly	+15min
Mooloolaba	-1hr 20min
Nerang River	+1hr
Noosa	-1hr 30min
Point Danger	-1hr 30min
Redcliffe	0
Redland Bay	+30min
Runaway Bay	-30min
Sanctuary Cove	+30min
Scarborough	+5min
Southport Broadwater	-35min
Tangalooma	-30min
Tin Can Bay	-45min
Toorbul	+30min
Tweed Heads	-45min
Urngan	-45min
Victoria Pt	+15min
Brunswick Heads	- 11hr 15min
Cabbage Tree Pt	+ 30min
Cape Moreton	- 1hr 15min
Jacobs Well	+ 14min
Peel Island	+12min
Rainbow Beach	- 1hr 20min
Tallebudgera Bridge	- 1hr 18min
Tewantin	- 15min

Day	Date	Tide 1	
Wed	1	3:52 AM	(1.39) H
THu	2	5:18 AM	(1.51) H
Fri	3	12:42 AM	(0.68) L
Sat	4	1:28 AM	(0.53) L
Sun	5	2:09 AM	(0.40) L
Mon	6	2:49 AM	(0.30) L
Tue	7	3:27 AM	(0.23) L
Wed	8	4:03 AM	(0.19) L
THu	9	4:39 AM	(0.20) L
Fri	10	5:15 AM	(0.25) L
Sat	11	5:52 AM	(0.35) L
Sun	12	12:35 AM	(1.66) H
Mon	13	1:43 AM	(1.50) H
Tue	14	3:14 AM	(1.44) H
Wed	15	4:44 AM	(1.52) H
THu	16	12:03 AM	(0.63) L
Fri	17	12:53 AM	(0.54) L
Sat	18	1:34 AM	(0.46) L
Sun	19	2:10 AM	(0.41) L
Mon	20	2:40 AM	(0.38) L
Tue	21 ●	3:08 AM	(0.35) L
Wed	22	3:34 AM	(0.34) L
THu	23	4:00 AM	(0.35) L
Fri	24	4:26 AM	(0.38) L
Sat	25	4:54 AM	(0.43) L
Sun	26	5:24 AM	(0.51) L
Mon	27	5:59 AM	(0.60) L
Tue	28	12:45 AM	(1.50) H
Wed	29	1:48 AM	(1.45) H
THu	30	3:16 AM	(1.47) H
Fri	31	4:39 AM	(1.59) H

Tide 2		Tide 3		Tide 4	
9:37 AM	(0.82) L	4:45 PM	(1.99) H	11:48 PM	(0.83) L
11:00 AM	(0.74) L	5:50 PM	(2.11) H		
6:17 AM	(1.68) H	12:09 PM	(0.61) L	6:43 PM	(2.25) H
7:08 AM	(1.86) H	1:07 PM	(0.49) L	7:28 PM	(2.36) H
7:54 AM	(2.03) H	2:00 PM	(0.40) L	8:11 PM	(2.42) H
8:39 AM	(2.18) H	2:52 PM	(0.34) L	8:52 PM	(2.41) H
9:23 AM	(2.32) H	3:41 PM	(0.32) L	9:33 PM	(2.35) H
10:08 AM	(2.42) H	4:30 PM	(0.35) L	10:15 PM	(2.22) H
10:53 AM	(2.48) H	5:20 PM	(0.42) L	10:58 PM	(2.05) H
11:41 AM	(2.48) H	6:13 PM	(0.53) L	11:43 PM	(1.85) H
12:30 PM	(2.42) H	7:12 PM	(0.65) L		
6:35 AM	(0.47) L	1:27 PM	(2.33) H	8:24 PM	(0.74) L
7:31 AM	(0.61) L	2:32 PM	(2.23) H	9:45 PM	(0.77) L
8:49 AM	(0.72) L	3:47 PM	(2.17) H	11:01 PM	(0.72) L
10:21 AM	(0.73) L	5:01 PM	(2.17) H		
5:52 AM	(1.67) H	11:39 AM	(0.67) L	6:03 PM	(2.20) H
6:45 AM	(1.84) H	12:41 PM	(0.60) L	6:54 PM	(2.22) H
7:30 AM	(1.98) H	1:32 PM	(0.54) L	7:36 PM	(2.21) H
8:09 AM	(2.09) H	2:16 PM	(0.52) L	8:13 PM	(2.18) H
8:45 AM	(2.18) H	2:58 PM	(0.52) L	8:46 PM	(2.12) H
9:18 AM	(2.24) H	3:35 PM	(0.54) L	9:17 PM	(2.05) H
9:50 AM	(2.29) H	4:12 PM	(0.57) L	9:47 PM	(1.97) H
10:23 AM	(2.30) H	4:47 PM	(0.61) L	10:17 PM	(1.88) H
10:55 AM	(2.29) H	5:21 PM	(0.66) L	10:48 PM	(1.78) H
11:29 AM	(2.25) H	5:57 PM	(0.73) L	11:21 PM	(1.68) H
12:04 PM	(2.19) H	6:36 PM	(0.80) L	11:59 PM	(1.59) H
12:45 PM	(2.12) H	7:25 PM	(0.87) L		
6:41 AM	(0.69) L	1:35 PM	(2.06) H	8:29 PM	(0.90) L
7:39 AM	(0.77) L	2:38 PM	(2.03) H	9:45 PM	(0.86) L
8:57 AM	(0.80) L	3:49 PM	(2.06) H	10:54 PM	(0.76) L
10:19 AM	(0.76) L	4:55 PM	(2.13) H	11:50 PM	(0.62) L

TIDE TIMES

Tim Smith's

POPULAR TIDE ADJUSTMENTS

Ballina	-1hr 10min
Bribie Island	-10min
Brunswick Heads	-1hr 20min
Bundaberg	-55min
Burleigh Heads	-1hr 30 min
Byron Bay	-1hr 20min
Caloundra	-1hr 25min
Cleveland	+15min
Coomera River	+1hr 30min
Donnybrook	+1hr
Fraser Island East	-1hr 20min
Gladstone	-20min
Gold Coast Seaway	-1hr 15min
Hervey Bay	+1hr
Jumpinpin	-1hr 30min
Manly	+15min
Mooloolaba	-1hr 20min
Nerang River	+1hr
Noosa	-1hr 30min
Point Danger	-1hr 30min
Redcliffe	0
Redland Bay	+30min
Runaway Bay	-30min
Sanctuary Cove	+30min
Scarborough	+5min
Southport Broadwater	-35min
Tangalooma	-30min
Tin Can Bay	-45min
Toorbul	+30min
Tweed Heads	-45min
Urngan	-45min
Victoria Pt	+15min
Brunswick Heads	- 11hr 15min
Cabbage Tree Pt	+ 30min
Cape Moreton	- 1hr 15min
Jacobs Well	+ 14min
Peel Island	+12min
Rainbow Beach	- 1hr 20min
Tallebudgera Bridge	- 1hr 18min
Tewantin	- 15min

Brisbane Bar

Day	Date		Tide 1	
Sat	1		5:44 AM	(1.77) **H**
Sun	2		12:40 AM	(0.48) L
Mon	3		1:26 AM	(0.35) L
Tue	4		2:09 AM	(0.26) L
Wed	5	◯	2:49 AM	(0.20) L
THu	6		3:29 AM	(0.18) L
Fri	7		4:08 AM	(0.20) L
Sat	8		4:48 AM	(0.26) L
Sun	9		5:31 AM	(0.36) L
Mon	10		12:34 AM	(1.62) **H**
Tue	11		1:41 AM	(1.54) **H**
Wed	12		2:56 AM	(1.54) **H**
THu	13		4:13 AM	(1.62) **H**
Fri	14		5:18 AM	(1.75) **H**
Sat	15		12:03 AM	(0.56) L
Sun	16		12:45 AM	(0.50) L
Mon	17		1:22 AM	(0.44) L
Tue	18		1:55 AM	(0.40) L
Wed	19		2:27 AM	(0.37) L
THu	20	●	2:57 AM	(0.36) L
Fri	21		3:27 AM	(0.37) L
Sat	22		3:57 AM	(0.40) L
Sun	23		4:29 AM	(0.44) L
Mon	24		5:02 AM	(0.50) L
Tue	25		5:40 AM	(0.56) L
Wed	26		12:34 AM	(1.60) **H**
THu	27		1:31 AM	(1.59) **H**
Fri	28		2:42 AM	(1.61) **H**
Sat	29		3:57 AM	(1.71) **H**
Sun	30		5:06 AM	(1.88) **H**

NOVEMBER 2025

Tide 2		Tide 3		Tide 4	
11:31 AM	(0.68) L	5:53 PM	(2.21) H		
6:38 AM	(1.98) H	12:37 PM	(0.58) L	6:44 PM	(2.26) H
7:28 AM	(2.18) H	1:38 PM	(0.50) L	7:32 PM	(2.26) H
8:15 AM	(2.36) H	2:35 PM	(0.44) L	8:19 PM	(2.21) H
9:02 AM	(2.50) H	3:30 PM	(0.41) L	9:06 PM	(2.12) H
9:49 AM	(2.60) H	4:23 PM	(0.41) L	9:55 PM	(2.00) H
10:37 AM	(2.64) H	5:17 PM	(0.45) L	10:45 PM	(1.87) H
11:27 AM	(2.62) H	6:14 PM	(0.52) L	11:37 PM	(1.73) H
12:17 PM	(2.54) H	7:15 PM	(0.60) L		
6:20 AM	(0.50) L	1:12 PM	(2.42) H	8:17 PM	(0.66) L
7:18 AM	(0.63) L	2:10 PM	(2.30) H	9:21 PM	(0.69) L
8:30 AM	(0.74) L	3:13 PM	(2.20) H	10:20 PM	(0.67) L
9:51 AM	(0.79) L	4:16 PM	(2.13) H	11:15 PM	(0.63) L
11:04 AM	(0.78) L	5:15 PM	(2.08) H		
6:13 AM	(1.91) H	12:09 PM	(0.75) L	6:07 PM	(2.05) H
7:00 AM	(2.05) H	1:03 PM	(0.71) L	6:52 PM	(2.01) H
7:40 AM	(2.17) H	1:52 PM	(0.68) L	7:33 PM	(1.97) H
8:17 AM	(2.27) H	2:37 PM	(0.65) L	8:11 PM	(1.92) H
8:53 AM	(2.34) H	3:18 PM	(0.63) L	8:46 PM	(1.87) H
9:28 AM	(2.38) H	3:58 PM	(0.63) L	9:21 PM	(1.82) H
10:01 AM	(2.39) H	4:35 PM	(0.65) L	9:55 PM	(1.77) H
10:35 AM	(2.37) H	5:11 PM	(0.68) L	10:30 PM	(1.72) H
11:10 AM	(2.34) H	5:48 PM	(0.72) L	11:06 PM	(1.68) H
11:46 AM	(2.30) H	6:28 PM	(0.76) L	11:47 PM	(1.64) H
12:27 PM	(2.25) H	7:13 PM	(0.78) L		
6:24 AM	(0.63) L	1:11 PM	(2.21) H	8:03 PM	(0.79) L
7:17 AM	(0.71) L	2:02 PM	(2.18) H	9:00 PM	(0.75) L
8:25 AM	(0.77) L	3:00 PM	(2.16) H	10:00 PM	(0.67) L
9:40 AM	(0.79) L	4:01 PM	(2.15) H	10:56 PM	(0.57) L
10:56 AM	(0.76) L	5:02 PM	(2.13) H	11:50 PM	(0.47) L

TIDE

TIMES

Tim Smith's

POPULAR TIDE ADJUSTMENTS

Ballina	-1hr 10min
Bribie Island	-10min
Brunswick Heads	-1hr 20min
Bundaberg	-55min
Burleigh Heads	-1hr 30 min
Byron Bay	-1hr 20min
Caloundra	-1hr 25min
Cleveland	+15min
Coomera River	+1hr 30min
Donnybrook	+1hr
Fraser Island East	-1hr 20min
Gladstone	-20min
Gold Coast Seaway	-1hr 15min
Hervey Bay	+1hr
Jumpinpin	-1hr 30min
Manly	+15min
Mooloolaba	-1hr 20min
Nerang River	+1hr
Noosa	-1hr 30min
Point Danger	-1hr 30min
Redcliffe	0
Redland Bay	+30min
Runaway Bay	-30min
Sanctuary Cove	+30min
Scarborough	+5min
Southport Broadwater	-35min
Tangalooma	-30min
Tin Can Bay	-45min
Toorbul	+30min
Tweed Heads	-45min
Urngan	-45min
Victoria Pt	+15min
Brunswick Heads	- 11hr 15min
Cabbage Tree Pt	+ 30min
Cape Moreton	- 1hr 15min
Jacobs Well	+ 14min
Peel Island	+12min
Rainbow Beach	- 1hr 20min
Tallebudgera Bridge	- 1hr 18min
Tewantin	- 15min

Brisbane Bar

Day	Date		Tide 1	
Mon	1		6:07 AM	(2.08) H
Tue	2		12:41 AM	(0.37) L
Wed	3		1:30 AM	(0.29) L
THu	4		2:17 AM	(0.25) L
Fri	5	○	3:03 AM	(0.22) L
Sat	6		3:48 AM	(0.24) L
Sun	7		4:34 AM	(0.28) L
Mon	8		5:21 AM	(0.37) L
Tue	9		12:25 AM	(1.71) H
Wed	10		1:19 AM	(1.69) H
THu	11		2:18 AM	(1.69) H
Fri	12		3:23 AM	(1.72) H
Sat	13		4:30 AM	(1.80) H
Sun	14		5:31 AM	(1.92) H
Mon	15		6:24 AM	(2.06) H
Tue	16		12:31 AM	(0.53) L
Wed	17		1:13 AM	(0.49) L
THu	18		1:51 AM	(0.45) L
Fri	19		2:29 AM	(0.43) L
Sat	20	●	3:04 AM	(0.42) L
Sun	21		3:39 AM	(0.42) L
Mon	22		4:15 AM	(0.43) L
Tue	23		4:51 AM	(0.45) L
Wed	24		5:30 AM	(0.50) L
THu	25		12:22 AM	(1.77) H
Fri	26		1:13 AM	(1.77) H
Sat	27		2:10 AM	(1.80) H
Sun	28		3:16 AM	(1.86) H
Mon	29		4:29 AM	(1.99) H
Tue	30		5:38 AM	(2.15) H
Wed	31		12:01 AM	(0.46) L

Tide 2		Tide 3		Tide 4	
12:09 PM	(0.71) L	6:01 PM	(2.10) H		
7:02 AM	(2.29) H	1:19 PM	(0.64) L	6:59 PM	(2.05) H
7:55 AM	(2.47) H	2:24 PM	(0.56) L	7:54 PM	(1.98) H
8:46 AM	(2.61) H	3:24 PM	(0.51) L	8:49 PM	(1.92) H
9:36 AM	(2.70) H	4:21 PM	(0.47) L	9:45 PM	(1.86) H
10:26 AM	(2.73) H	5:16 PM	(0.47) L	10:38 PM	(1.80) H
11:15 AM	(2.70) H	6:10 PM	(0.50) L	11:31 PM	(1.75) H
12:03 PM	(2.61) H	7:01 PM	(0.55) L		
6:10 AM	(0.48) L	12:51 PM	(2.50) H	7:51 PM	(0.60) L
7:01 AM	(0.61) L	1:39 PM	(2.36) H	8:39 PM	(0.64) L
8:00 AM	(0.74) L	2:28 PM	(2.21) H	9:26 PM	(0.66) L
9:05 AM	(0.85) L	3:19 PM	(2.08) H	10:13 PM	(0.65) L
10:16 AM	(0.91) L	4:14 PM	(1.96) H	11:00 PM	(0.62) L
11:28 AM	(0.92) L	5:10 PM	(1.87) H	11:46 PM	(0.58) L
12:33 PM	(0.89) L	6:04 PM	(1.82) H		
7:10 AM	(2.18) H	1:30 PM	(0.82) L	6:55 PM	(1.78) H
7:52 AM	(2.29) H	2:19 PM	(0.76) L	7:42 PM	(1.76) H
8:31 AM	(2.36) H	3:04 PM	(0.71) L	8:24 PM	(1.75) H
9:09 AM	(2.41) H	3:45 PM	(0.68) L	9:03 PM	(1.75) H
9:45 AM	(2.43) H	4:25 PM	(0.67) L	9:41 PM	(1.76) H
10:21 AM	(2.43) H	5:01 PM	(0.67) L	10:17 PM	(1.76) H
10:57 AM	(2.43) H	5:38 PM	(0.68) L	10:57 PM	(1.77) H
11:32 AM	(2.42) H	6:15 PM	(0.68) L	11:38 PM	(1.77) H
12:09 PM	(2.40) H	6:55 PM	(0.68) L		
6:13 AM	(0.57) L	12:47 PM	(2.36) H	7:35 PM	(0.67) L
7:01 AM	(0.65) L	1:30 PM	(2.30) H	8:19 PM	(0.64) L
7:59 AM	(0.74) L	2:17 PM	(2.21) H	9:09 PM	(0.60) L
9:08 AM	(0.82) L	3:14 PM	(2.10) H	10:03 PM	(0.56) L
10:26 AM	(0.86) L	4:19 PM	(1.98) H	11:01 PM	(0.51) L
11:49 AM	(0.84) L	5:29 PM	(1.89) H		
6:43 AM	(2.33) H	1:11 PM	(0.76) L	6:37 PM	(1.83) H

SOLAR/LUNAR BITE TIMES

Apogee moon phase on Tuesday 10th
Perigee moon phase on Thursday 26th
● **New moon on Sunday 15th**
First quarter moon on Sunday 22nd
○ **Full moon on Sunday 29th**
Last quarter moon phase on Sunday 7th

Brisbane, QLD: Rise: 05:10am Set: 05:50pm
(Note: These sun rise/set times are averages for the month)

DAY	MINOR BITE	MAJOR BITE	MINOR BITE	MAJOR BITE	SALT WATER RATING	FRESH WATER RATING
SUN 1	7:39 PM	12:12 AM	5:49 AM	12:37 PM	7	6
MON 2	8:52 PM	1:03 AM	6:19 AM	1:29 PM	5	5
TUE 3	10:03 PM	1:56 AM	6:53 AM	2:22 PM	4	4
WED 4	11:09 PM	2:50 AM	7:32 AM	3:17 PM	3	6
THUR 5		3:45 AM	8:18 AM	4:12 PM	4	4
FRI 6	12:10 AM	4:40 AM	9:10 AM	5:07 PM	5	5
SAT 7	1:01 AM	5:34 AM	10:08 AM	5:59 PM	5	5
SUN 8	1:45 AM	6:24 AM	11:08 AM	6:48 PM	6	6
MON 9	2:20 AM	7:12 AM	12:10 PM	7:34 PM	7	7
TUE 10	2:50 AM	7:57 AM	1:10 PM	8:18 PM	7	8
WED 11	3:16 AM	8:39 AM	2:10 PM	8:59 PM	5	8

POPULAR LOCATION ADJUSTMENTS (See full list on page 7)

DAY	MINOR BITE	MAJOR BITE	MINOR BITE	MAJOR BITE	SALT WATER RATING	FRESH WATER RATING
THUR 12	3:39 AM	9:20 AM	3:09 PM	9:40 PM	6	7
FRI 13	4:01 AM	10:00 AM	4:08 PM	10:19 PM	8	8
SAT 14	4:22 AM	10:40 AM	5:07 PM	11:00 PM	8	8
SUN 15	4:44 AM	11:21 AM	6:09 PM	11:42 PM ●	8	8
MON 16	5:08 AM	12:05 PM	7:12 PM		8	6
TUE 17	5:37 AM	12:52 PM	8:19 PM	12:28 AM	7	6
WED 18	6:10 AM	1:44 PM	9:27 PM	1:18 AM	6	7
THUR 19	6:51 AM	2:39 PM	10:33 PM	2:11 AM	5	5
FRI 20	7:42 AM	3:38 PM	11:35 PM	3:08 AM	4	6
SAT 21	8:43 AM	4:39 PM		4:08 AM	3	5
SUN 22	9:52 AM	5:38 PM	12:30 AM	5:08 AM	4	6
MON 23	11:05 AM	6:35 PM	1:15 AM	6:06 AM	5	6
TUE 24	12:20 PM	7:29 PM	1:53 AM	7:01 AM	4	5
WED 25	1:35 PM	8:20 PM	2:25 AM	7:54 AM	3	5
THUR 26	2:48 PM	9:10 PM	2:53 AM	8:45 AM	6	6
FRI 27	4:00 PM	9:59 PM	3:20 AM	9:34 AM	5	7
SAT 28	5:13 PM	10:49 PM	3:47 AM	10:24 AM	3	8
SUN 29	6:26 PM	11:41 PM	4:15 AM	11:15 AM ○	5	7
MON 30	7:39 PM		4:47 AM	12:07 PM	7	6
TUE 31	8:50 PM	12:35 AM	5:24 AM	1:03 PM	7	6

SOLAR/LUNAR

BITE TIMES

Tim Smith's

Apogee moon phase on Tuesday 7th
Perigee moon phase on Wednesday 22nd
● New moon on Monday 13th
First quarter moon on Monday 20th
○ Full moon on Monday 27th
Last quarter moon phase on Sunday 5th

Brisbane, QLD: Rise: 04:40am Set: 06:10pm
(Note: These sun rise/set times are averages for the month)

DAY	MINOR BITE	MAJOR BITE	MINOR BITE	MAJOR BITE	SALT WATER RATING	FRESH WATER RATING
WED 1	9:55 PM	1:31 AM	6:08 AM	1:58 PM	5	5
THUR 2	10:52 PM	2:27 AM	6:58 AM	2:54 PM	4	4
FRI 3	11:40 PM	3:23 AM	7:55 AM	3:49 PM	3	6
SAT 4		4:16 AM	8:56 AM	4:41 PM	4	4
SUN 5	12:19 AM	5:06 AM	9:58 AM	5:29 PM	5	5
MON 6	12:51 AM	5:52 AM	10:59 AM	6:13 PM	6	6
TUE 7	1:19 AM	6:35 AM	11:59 AM	6:55 PM	7	7
WED 8	1:42 AM	7:16 AM	12:58 PM	7:36 PM	7	7
THUR 9	2:04 AM	7:56 AM	1:56 PM	8:15 PM	7	8
FRI 10	2:26 AM	8:36 AM	2:56 PM	8:56 PM	5	8
SAT 11	2:47 AM	9:17 AM	3:56 PM	9:38 PM	6	7

NOVEMBER 2024

POPULAR LOCATION ADJUSTMENTS (See full list on page 7)

See full list on page 7

DAY	MINOR BITE	MAJOR BITE	MINOR BITE	MAJOR BITE	SALT WATER RATING	FRESH WATER RATING
SUN 12	3:11 AM	10:00 AM	5:00 PM	10:23 PM	8	8
MON 13	3:38 AM	10:47 AM	6:06 PM	11:11 PM ●	8	8
TUE 14	4:10 AM	11:37 AM	7:15 PM		8	6
WED 15	4:49 AM	12:33 PM	8:24 PM	12:05 AM	7	6
THUR 16	5:37 AM	1:32 PM	9:29 PM	1:02 AM	6	7
FRI 17	6:36 AM	2:33 PM	10:26 PM	2:02 AM	5	5
SAT 18	7:43 AM	3:33 PM	11:15 PM	3:02 AM	4	6
SUN 19	8:56 AM	4:31 PM	11:54 PM	4:01 AM	3	5
MON 20	10:10 AM	5:25 PM		4:58 AM	4	6
TUE 21	11:23 AM	6:15 PM	12:27 AM	5:49 AM	5	6
WED 22	12:34 PM	7:04 PM	12:56 AM	6:39 AM	4	5
THUR 23	1:44 PM	7:52 PM	1:22 AM	7:28 AM	3	5
FRI 24	2:55 PM	8:40 PM	1:48 AM	8:16 AM	6	6
SAT 25	4:06 PM	9:29 PM	2:15 AM	9:04 AM	5	7
SUN 26	5:17 PM	10:21 PM	2:44 AM	9:54 AM	3	8
MON 27	6:29 PM	11:16 PM	3:18 AM	10:48 AM ○	5	7
TUE 28	7:37 PM		3:58 AM	11:44 AM	7	6
WED 29	8:38 PM	12:13 AM	4:46 AM	12:41 PM	7	6
THUR 30	9:31 PM	1:10 AM	5:41 AM	1:37 PM	7	6

SOLAR/LUNAR BITE TIMES

Apogee moon phase on Tuesday 5th
Perigee moon phase on Sunday 17th
● New moon on Wednesday 13th
First quarter moon on Wednesday 20th
○ Full moon on Wednesday 27th
Last quarter moon phase on Tuesday 5th

Brisbane, QLD: Rise: 04:40am Set: 06:30pm
(Note: These sun rise/set times are averages for the month)

DAY	MINOR BITE	MAJOR BITE	MINOR BITE	MAJOR BITE	SALT WATER RATING	FRESH WATER RATING
FRI 1	10:14 PM	2:05 AM	6:41 AM	2:31 PM	5	5
SAT 2	10:50 PM	2:57 AM	7:43 AM	3:20 PM	4	4
SUN 3	11:19 PM	3:45 AM	8:46 AM	4:07 PM	3	6
MON 4	11:44 PM	4:29 AM	9:47 AM	4:49 PM	4	4
TUE 5		5:11 AM	10:46 AM	5:30 PM	5	5
WED 6	12:07 AM	5:51 AM	11:44 AM	6:11 PM	6	6
THUR 7	12:28 AM	6:31 AM	12:42 PM	6:51 PM	7	7
FRI 8	12:49 AM	7:11 AM	1:42 PM	7:31 PM	7	8
SAT 9	1:12 AM	7:52 AM	2:43 PM	8:14 PM	7	8
SUN 10	1:37 AM	8:37 AM	3:48 PM	9:01 PM	5	8
MON 11	2:07 AM	9:26 AM	4:57 PM	9:52 PM	6	7

DAY	MINOR BITE	MAJOR BITE	MINOR BITE	MAJOR BITE	SALT WATER RATING	FRESH WATER RATING
TUE 12	2:43 AM	10:20 AM	6:07 PM	10:49 PM	8	8
WED 13	3:28 AM	11:19 AM	7:15 PM	11:49 PM ●	8	8
THUR 14	4:24 AM	12:21 PM	8:17 PM		8	6
FRI 15	5:31 AM	1:24 PM	9:10 PM	12:52 AM	7	6
SAT 16	6:44 AM	2:24 PM	9:54 PM	1:53 AM	6	7
SUN 17	8:00 AM	3:21 PM	10:29 PM	2:52 AM	5	5
MON 18	9:14 AM	4:13 PM	10:59 PM	3:46 AM	4	6
TUE 19	10:26 AM	5:02 PM	11:26 PM	4:37 AM	3	5
WED 20	11:36 AM	5:49 PM	11:52 PM	5:25 AM	4	6
THUR 21	12:45 PM	6:36 PM		6:12 AM	5	6
FRI 22	1:54 PM	7:24 PM	12:17 AM	7:00 AM	4	5
SAT 23	3:04 PM	8:14 PM	12:45 AM	7:48 AM	3	5
SUN 24	4:14 PM	9:07 PM	1:17 AM	8:40 AM	6	6
MON 25	5:22 PM	10:02 PM	1:54 AM	9:34 AM	5	7
TUE 26	6:25 PM	10:58 PM	2.30 AM	10:30 AM	3	8
WED 27	7:21 PM	11:54 PM	3:29 AM	11:26 AM ○	5	7
THUR 28	8:08 PM		4:27 AM	12:20 PM	7	6
FRI 29	8:47 PM	12:47 AM	5:29 AM	1:11 PM	7	6
SAT 30	9:19 PM	1:37 AM	6:32 AM	2:00 PM	5	5
SUN 31	9:46 PM	2:23 AM	7:34 AM	2:44 PM	5	5

SOLAR/LUNAR
BITE TIMES

Apogee moon phase on Tuesday 21st
Perigee moon phase on Wednesday 8th
● **New moon on Wednesday 29th**
First quarter moon on Tuesday 7th
○ **Full moon on Tuesday 14th**
Last quarter moon phase on Wednesday 22nd

Brisbane, QLD: Rise: 05:00am Set: 06:40pm

(Note: These sun rise/set times are averages for the month)

DAY	MINOR BITE	MAJOR BITE	MINOR BITE	MAJOR BITE	SALT WATER RATING	FRESH WATER RATING
WED 1	4:44 AM	12:31 PM	8:10 PM	12:02 AM	8	6
THUR 2	5:54 AM	1:26 PM	8:47 PM	12:58 AM	7	6
FRI 3	7:06 AM	2:18 PM	9:18 PM	1:52 AM	6	7
SAT 4	8:17 AM	3:07 PM	9:46 PM	2:42 AM	5	5
SUN 5	9:27 AM	3:55 PM	10:11 PM	3:30 AM	4	6
MON 6	10:37 AM	4:42 PM	10:36 PM	4:18 AM	3	5
TUE 7	11:47 AM	5:30 PM	11:03 PM	5:05 AM	4	6
WED 8	12:59 PM	6:20 PM	11:33 PM	5:55 AM	5	6
THUR 9	2:13 PM	7:14 PM		6:46 AM	4	5
FRI 10	3:27 PM	8:12 PM	12:08 AM	7:43 AM	3	5
SAT 11	4:39 PM	9:13 PM	12:52 AM	8:42 AM	6	6

POPULAR LOCATION ADJUSTMENTS (See full list on page 7)

DAY	MINOR BITE	MAJOR BITE	MINOR BITE	MAJOR BITE	SALT WATER RATING	FRESH WATER RATING
SUN 12	5:43 PM	10:14 PM	1:44 AM	9:43 AM	5	7
MON 13	6:38 PM	11:14 PM	2:46 AM	10:43 AM	3	8
TUE 14	7:22 PM		3:54 AM	11:41 AM ○	5	7
WED 15	7:57 PM	12:09 AM	5:03 AM	12:34 PM	7	6
THUR 16	8:26 PM	1:00 AM	6:11 AM	1:23 PM	7	6
FRI 17	8:50 PM	1:47 AM	7:16 AM	2:07 PM	5	5
SAT 18	9:12 PM	2:29 AM	8:18 AM	2:49 PM	4	4
SUN 19	9:33 PM	3:10 AM	9:17 AM	3:29 PM	3	6
MON 20	9:54 PM	3:49 AM	10:15 AM	4:08 PM	3	6
TUE 21	10:16 PM	4:29 AM	11:13 AM	4:48 PM	4	4
WED 22	10:41 PM	5:09 AM	12:13 PM	5:30 PM	5	5
THUR 23	11:10 PM	5:52 AM	1:14 PM	6:15 PM	6	6
FRI 24	11:46 PM	6:39 AM	2:17 PM	7:03 PM	7	7
SAT 25		7:29 AM	3:20 PM	7:56 PM	7	8
SUN 26	12:29 AM	8:23 AM	4:20 PM	8:51 PM	5	8
MON 27	1:23 AM	9:20 AM	5:15 PM	9:48 PM	6	7
TUE 28	2:26 AM	10:18 AM	6:03 PM	10:46 PM	8	8
WED 29	3:35 AM	11:15 AM	6:44 PM	11:41 PM ●	8	8
THUR 30	4:48 AM	12:09 PM	7:18 PM		8	6
FRI 31	6:02 AM	1:01 PM	7:47 PM	12:35 AM	7	6

SOLAR/LUNAR BITE TIMES

Apogee moon phase on Tuesday 18th
Perigee moon phase on Sunday 2nd
● New moon on Friday 28th
First quarter moon on Wednesday 5th
○ Full moon on Thursday 13th
Last quarter moon phase on Friday 21st

Brisbane, QLD: Rise: 05:30am Set: 06:30pm
(Note: These sun rise/set times are averages for the month)

DAY	MINOR BITE	MAJOR BITE	MINOR BITE	MAJOR BITE	SALT WATER RATING	FRESH WATER RATING
SAT 1	7:15 AM	1:50 PM	8:14 PM	1:25 AM	6	7
SUN 2	8:26 AM	2:39 PM	8:40 PM	2:14 AM	5	5
MON 3	9:38 AM	3:27 PM	9:06 PM	3:02 AM	4	6
TUE 4	10:50 AM	4:17 PM	9:35 PM	3:52 AM	3	5
WED 5	12:04 PM	5:10 PM	10:09 PM	4:43 AM	4	6
THUR 6	1:18 PM	6:06 PM	10:49 PM	5:38 AM	5	6
FRI 7	2:29 PM	7:05 PM	11:37 PM	6:35 AM	4	5
SAT 8	3:35 PM	8:05 PM		7:34 AM	3	5
SUN 9	4:32 PM	9:04 PM	12:35 AM	8:34 AM	6	6
MON 10	5:18 PM	10:00 PM	1:40 AM	9:31 AM	5	7

DAY	MINOR BITE	MAJOR BITE	MINOR BITE	MAJOR BITE	SALT WATER RATING	FRESH WATER RATING
TUE 11	5:56 PM	10:52 PM	2:48 AM	10:26 AM	3	8
WED 12	6:26 PM	11:40 PM	3:56 AM	11:16 AM	5	7
THUR 13	6:52 PM		5:01 AM	12:01 PM	○ 5	7
FRI 14	7:15 PM	12:24 AM	6:04 AM	12:44 PM	7	6
SAT 15	7:36 PM	1:05 AM	7:05 AM	1:24 PM	7	6
SUN 16	7:57 PM	1:45 AM	8:04 AM	2:04 PM	5	5
MON 17	8:18 PM	2:24 AM	9:02 AM	2:43 PM	4	4
TUE 18	8:42 PM	3:04 AM	10:01 AM	3:24 PM	3	6
WED 19	9:09 PM	3:46 AM	11:01 AM	4:08 PM	4	4
THUR 20	9:41 PM	4:31 AM	12:03 PM	4:55 PM	4	4
FRI 21	10:20 PM	5:19 AM	1:05 PM	5:45 PM	5	5
SAT 22	11:08 PM	6:11 AM	2:06 PM	6:37 PM	6	6
SUN 23		7:05 AM	3:03 PM	7:33 PM	7	7
MON 24	12:06 AM	8:02 AM	3:53 PM	8:30 PM	7	8
TUE 25	1:12 AM	8:59 AM	4:37 PM	9:26 PM	5	8
WED 26	2:23 AM	9:54 AM	5:14 PM	10:21 PM	6	7
THUR 27	3:38 AM	10:48 AM	5:45 PM	11:13 PM	8	8
FRI 28	4:52 AM	11:39 AM	6:14 PM		● 8	8

SOLAR/LUNAR BITE TIMES

Tim Smith's

Apogee moon phase on Tuesday 18th
Perigee moon phase on Sunday 2nd and Sunday 30th
● New moon on Saturday 29th
First quarter moon on Friday 7th
○ Full moon on Friday 14th
Last quarter moon phase on Saturday 22nd

Brisbane, QLD: Rise: 05:40am Set: 06:00pm

(Note: These sun rise/set times are averages for the month)

DAY	MINOR BITE	MAJOR BITE	MINOR BITE	MAJOR BITE	SALT WATER RATING	FRESH WATER RATING
SAT 1	6:06 AM	12:29 PM	6:41 PM	12:04 AM	8	6
SUN 2	7:20 AM	1:19 PM	7:07 PM	12:54 AM	7	6
MON 3	8:35 AM	2:10 PM	7:36 PM	1:44 AM	6	7
TUE 4	9:51 AM	3:04 PM	8:09 PM	2:37 AM	5	5
WED 5	11:07 AM	4:00 PM	8:47 PM	3:31 AM	4	6
THUR 6	12:21 PM	4:59 PM	9:34 PM	4:29 AM	3	5
FRI 7	1:29 PM	6:00 PM	10:29 PM	5:29 AM	4	6
SAT 8	2:29 PM	6:59 PM	11:31 PM	6:29 AM	5	6
SUN 9	3:18 PM	7:56 PM		7:27 AM	4	5
MON 10	3:57 PM	8:48 PM	12:38 AM	8:22 AM	3	5
TUE 11	4:29 PM	9:36 PM	1:45 AM	9:11 AM	6	6

MARCH 2025
POPULAR LOCATION (See full list)
ADJUSTMENTS (on page 7)

DAY	MINOR BITE	MAJOR BITE	MINOR BITE	MAJOR BITE	SALT WATER RATING	FRESH WATER RATING
WED 12	4:56 PM	10:21 PM	2:51 AM	9:58 AM	5	7
THUR 13	5:19 PM	11:02 PM	3:54 AM	10:41 AM	3	8
FRI 14	5:40 PM	11:42 PM	4:55 AM	11:22 AM ○	5	7
SAT 15	6:01 PM		5:54 AM	12:01 PM	7	6
SUN 16	6:22 PM	12:22 AM	6:52 AM	12:41 PM	7	6
MON 17	6:45 PM	1:02 AM	7:51 AM	1:22 PM	7	6
TUE 18	7:10 PM	1:43 AM	8:51 AM	2:04 PM	5	5
WED 19	7:40 PM	2:26 AM	9:52 AM	2:49 PM	4	4
THUR 20	8:16 PM	3:13 AM	10:54 AM	3:37 PM	3	6
FRI 21	9:00 PM	4:02 AM	11:54 AM	4:28 PM	4	4
SAT 22	9:52 PM	4:55 AM	12:52 PM	5:22 PM	5	5
SUN 23	10:53 PM	5:49 AM	1:44 PM	6:17 PM	6	6
MON 24		6:45 AM	2:29 PM	7:11 PM	7	7
TUE 25	12:00 AM	7:39 AM	3:08 PM	8:06 PM	7	8
WED 26	1:12 AM	8:33 AM	3:41 PM	8:58 PM	5	8
THUR 27	2:25 AM	9:24 AM	4:11 PM	9:49 PM	6	7
FRI 28	3:39 AM	10:15 AM	4:38 PM	10:40 PM	8	8
SAT 29	4:53 AM	11:05 AM	5:05 PM	11:30 PM ●	8	8
SUN 30	6:09 AM	11:57 AM	5:33 PM		8	6
MON 31	7:27 AM	12:51 PM	6:05 PM	12:24 AM	7	6

SOLAR/LUNAR BITE TIMES

Apogee moon phase on Monday 14th
Perigee moon phase on Monday 28th
● **New moon on Monday 28th**
First quarter moon on Saturday 5th
○ **Full moon on Sunday 13th**
Last quarter moon phase on Monday 21st

Brisbane, QLD: Rise: 06:00am Set: 05:30pm
(Note: These sun rise/set times are averages for the month)

DAY	MINOR BITE	MAJOR BITE	MINOR BITE	MAJOR BITE	SALT WATER RATING	FRESH WATER RATING
TUE 1	8:45 AM	1:48 PM	6:43 PM	1:19 AM	6	7
WED 2	10:04 AM	2:48 PM	7:27 PM	2:17 AM	5	5
THUR 3	11:18 AM	3:50 PM	8:21 PM	3:19 AM	4	6
FRI 4	12:23 PM	4:52 PM	9:23 PM	4:20 AM	3	5
SAT 5	1:16 PM	5:51 PM	10:30 PM	5:21 AM	4	6
SUN 6	1:58 PM	6:45 PM	11:38 PM	6:17 AM	5	6
MON 7	2:32 PM	7:34 PM		7:09 AM	4	5
TUE 8	3:00 PM	8:20 PM	12:44 AM	7:57 AM	3	5
WED 9	3:24 PM	9:02 PM	1:47 AM	8:41 AM	6	6
THUR 10	3:46 PM	9:42 PM	2:48 AM	9:22 AM	6	6
FRI 11	4:07 PM	10:21 PM	3:47 AM	10:01 AM	5	7

APRIL 2025
POPULAR LOCATION (See full list)
ADJUSTMENTS (on page 7)

DAY	MINOR BITE	MAJOR BITE	MINOR BITE	MAJOR BITE	SALT WATER RATING	FRESH WATER RATING
SAT 12	4:27 PM	11:00 PM	4:45 AM	10:40 AM	3	8
SUN 13	4:49 PM	11:41 PM	5:44 AM	11:20 AM ○	5	7
MON 14	5:14 PM		6:43 AM	12:02 PM	7	6
TUE 15	5:42 PM	12:24 AM	7:44 AM	12:46 PM	7	6
WED 16	6:16 PM	1:09 AM	8:45 AM	1:33 PM	5	5
THUR 17	6:57 PM	1:57 AM	9:46 AM	2:22 PM	4	4
FRI 18	7:45 PM	2:49 AM	10:45 AM	3:15 PM	4	4
SAT 19	8:42 PM	3:42 AM	11:38 AM	4:08 PM	3	6
SUN 20	9:46 PM	4:36 AM	12:25 PM	5:03 PM	4	4
MON 21	10:54 PM	5:30 AM	1:05 PM	5:56 PM	5	5
TUE 22		6:22 AM	1:39 PM	6:47 PM	6	6
WED 23	12:04 AM	7:12 AM	2:09 PM	7:36 PM	7	7
THUR 24	1.15 AM	8:01 AM	2:36 PM	8:25 PM	7	8
FRI 25	2:27 AM	8:50 AM	3:03 PM	9:15 PM	5	8
SAT 26	3:40 AM	9:41 AM	3:30 PM	10:07 PM	6	7
SUN 27	4:56 AM	10:33 AM	3:59 PM	11:00 PM	8	8
MON 28	6:16 AM	11:29 AM	4:34 PM	11:59 PM ●	8	8
TUE 29	7:36 AM	12:30 PM	5:16 PM		8	6
WED 30	8:55 AM	1:33 PM	6: 7 PM	1: 1 AM	7	6

BITE TIMES

Tim Smith's

Apogee moon phase on Sunday 11th
Perigee moon phase on Monday 26th
● **New moon on Tuesday 27th**
First quarter moon on Sunday 4th
○ **Full moon on Tuesday 13th**
Last quarter moon phase on Tuesday 20th

Brisbane, QLD: Rise: 06:20am Set: 05:00pm

(Note: These sun rise/set times are averages for the month)

DAY	MINOR BITE	MAJOR BITE	MINOR BITE	MAJOR BITE	SALT WATER RATING	FRESH WATER RATING
THUR 1	10:07 AM	2:38 PM	7:09 PM	2:05 AM	6	7
FRI 2	11:07 AM	3:40 PM	8:16 PM	3:08 AM	5	5
SAT 3	11:55 AM	4:38 PM	9:26 PM	4:09 AM	4	6
SUN 4	12:33 PM	5:30 PM	10:34 PM	5:03 AM	3	5
MON 5	1:04 PM	6:18 PM	11:40 PM	5:54 AM	4	6
TUE 6	1:29 PM	7:01 PM		6:39 AM	5	6
WED 7	1:51 PM	7:42 PM	12:42 AM	7:21 AM	4	5
THUR 8	2:12 PM	8:21 PM	1:41 AM	8:01 AM	3	5
FRI 9	2:33 PM	9:00 PM	2:39 AM	8:40 AM	6	6
SAT 10	2:54 PM	9:40 PM	3:37 AM	9:20 AM	5	7
SUN 11	3:18 PM	10:22 PM	4:36 AM	10:01 AM	3	8

DAY	MINOR BITE	MAJOR BITE	MINOR BITE	MAJOR BITE	SALT WATER RATING	FRESH WATER RATING
MON 12	3:45 PM	11:07 PM	5:36 AM	10:44 AM	3	8
TUE 13	4:17 PM	11:54 PM	6:38 AM	11:30 AM	○ 5	7
WED 14	4:56 PM		7:39 AM	12:19 PM	7	6
THUR 15	5:42 PM	12:45 AM	8:39 AM	1:11 PM	7	6
FRI 16	6:37 PM	1:38 AM	9:34 AM	2:05 PM	5	5
SAT 17	7:38 PM	2:32 AM	10:22 AM	2:58 PM	4	4
SUN 18	8:44 PM	3:25 AM	11:04 AM	3:50 PM	3	6
MON 19	9:51 PM	4:17 AM	11:39 AM	4:41 PM	4	4
TUE 20	11:00 PM	5:06 AM	12:10 PM	5:30 PM	5	5
WED 21		5:54 AM	12:37 PM	6:17 PM	6	6
THUR 22	12:09 AM	6:41 AM	1:03 PM	7:04 PM	7	7
FRI 23	1:19 AM	7:29 AM	1:28 PM	7:53 PM	7	8
SAT 24	2:31 AM	8:19 AM	1:56 PM	8:45 PM	5	8
SUN 25	3:47 AM	9:12 AM	2:27 PM	9:40 PM	6	7
MON 26	5:06 AM	10:09 AM	3:05 PM	10:40 PM	0	8
TUE 27	6:26 AM	11:11 AM	3:51 PM	11:44 PM	● 8	8
WED 28	7:43 AM	12:17 PM	4:49 PM		8	6
THUR 29	8:50 AM	1:22 PM	5:55 PM	12:49 AM	7	6
FRI 30	9:46 AM	2:24 PM	7:07 PM	1:53 AM	6	7
SAT 31	10:29 AM	3:20 PM	8:18 PM	2:52 AM	5	5

SOLAR/LUNAR

BITE TIMES

Tim Smith's

Apogee moon phase on Saturday 7th
Perigee moon phase on Monday 23rd
● **New moon on Wednesday 25th**
First quarter moon on Tuesday 3rd
○ **Full moon on Wednesday 11th**
Last quarter moon phase on Thursday 19th

Brisbane, QLD: Rise: 06:30am Set: 05:00pm

(Note: These sun rise/set times are averages for the month)

DAY	MINOR BITE	MAJOR BITE	MINOR BITE	MAJOR BITE	SALT WATER RATING	FRESH WATER RATING
SUN 1	11:03 AM	4:11 PM	9:27 PM	3:45 AM	4	6
MON 2	11:31 AM	4:57 PM	10:32 PM	4:33 AM	3	5
TUE 3	11:55 AM	5:39 PM	11:33 PM	5:17 AM	4	6
WED 4	12:17 PM	6:19 PM		5:59 AM	5	6
THUR 5	12:37 PM	6:59 PM	12:32 AM	6:39 AM	4	5
FRI 6	12:59 PM	7:39 PM	1:30 AM	7:18 AM	3	5
SAT 7	1:22 PM	8:20 PM	2:28 AM	7:59 AM	3	5
SUN 8	1:47 PM	9:03 PM	3:28 AM	8:41 AM	6	6
MON 9	2:18 PM	9:50 PM	4:29 AM	9:26 AM	5	7
TUE 10	2:55 PM	10:40 PM	5:31 AM	10:15 AM	3	8
WED 11	3:39 PM	11:33 PM	6:32 AM	11:06 AM	○ 5	7

DAY	MINOR BITE	MAJOR BITE	MINOR BITE	MAJOR BITE	SALT WATER RATING	FRESH WATER RATING
THUR 12	4:31 PM		7:29 AM	12:00 PM	7	6
FRI 13	5:31 PM	12:27 AM	8:20 AM	12:54 PM	7	6
SAT 14	6:36 PM	1:21 AM	9:04 AM	1:47 PM	5	5
SUN 15	7:44 PM	2:14 AM	9:41 AM	2:39 PM	4	4
MON 16	8:52 PM	3:04 AM	10:12 AM	3:28 PM	4	4
TUE 17	9:59 PM	3:52 AM	10:40 AM	4:15 PM	3	6
WED 18	11:07 PM	4:38 AM	11:05 AM	5:00 PM	4	4
THUR 19		5:24 AM	11:30 AM	5:47 PM	5	5
FRI 20	12:17 AM	6:11 AM	11:56 AM	6:36 PM	6	6
SAT 21	1:28 AM	7:01 AM	12:25 PM	7:27 PM	7	7
SUN 22	2:43 AM	7:55 AM	12:58 PM	8:23 PM	7	8
MON 23	4:01 AM	8:53 AM	1:40 PM	9:24 PM	6	7
TUE 24	5:18 AM	9:56 AM	2:31 PM	10:28 PM	8	8
WED 25	6:30 AM	11:01 AM	3:33 PM	11:33 PM ●	8	8
THUR 26	7:31 AM	12:05 PM	4:43 PM		8	6
FRI 27	8:20 AM	1:05 PM	5:57 PM	12:35 AM	7	6
SAT 28	8:59 AM	2:00 PM	7:08 PM	1:32 AM	6	7
SUN 29	9:30 AM	2:49 PM	8:16 PM	2:24 AM	6	7
MON 30	9:56 AM	3:34 PM	9:2 PM	3:11 AM	5	5

SOLAR/LUNAR BITE TIMES

Apogee moon phase on Saturday 5th
Perigee moon phase on Sunday 20th
● **New moon on Friday 25th**
First quarter moon on Thursday 3rd
○ **Full moon on Friday 11th**
Last quarter moon phase on Friday 18th

Brisbane, QLD: Rise: 06:30am Set: 05:10pm

(Note: These sun rise/set times are averages for the month)

DAY	MINOR BITE	MAJOR BITE	MINOR BITE	MAJOR BITE	SALT WATER RATING	FRESH WATER RATING
TUE 1	10:19 AM	4:15 PM	10:21 PM	3:54 AM	4	6
WED 2	10:40 AM	4:56 PM	11:20 PM	4:35 AM	3	5
THUR 3	11:02 AM	5:35 PM		5:15 AM	4	6
FRI 4	11:24 AM	6:16 PM	12:19 AM	5:55 AM	5	6
SAT 5	11:49 AM	6:59 PM	1:18 AM	6:37 AM	4	5
SUN 6	12:18 PM	7:45 PM	2:19 AM	7:21 AM	3	5
MON 7	12:52 PM	8:33 PM	3:21 AM	8:09 AM	6	6
TUE 8	1:33 PM	9:25 PM	4:22 AM	8:58 AM	5	7
WED 9	2:23 PM	10:20 PM	5:21 AM	9:52 AM	5	7
THUR 10	3:22 PM	11:14 PM	6:14 AM	10:46 AM	3	8
FRI 11	4:26 PM		7:01 AM	11:41 AM	○ 5	7

DAY	MINOR BITE	MAJOR BITE	MINOR BITE	MAJOR BITE	SALT WATER RATING	FRESH WATER RATING
SAT 12	5:34 PM	12:08 AM	7:41 AM	12:33 PM	7	6
SUN 13	6:43 PM	1:00 AM	8:15 AM	1:24 PM	7	6
MON 14	7:52 PM	1:49 AM	8:44 AM	2:13 PM	5	5
TUE 15	9:00 PM	2:37 AM	9:10 AM	3:00 PM	4	4
WED 16	10:08 PM	3:23 AM	9:34 AM	3:46 PM	3	6
THUR 17	11:18 PM	4:09 AM	9:59 AM	4:33 PM	4	4
FRI 18		4:57 AM	10:26 AM	5:22 PM	5	5
SAT 19	12:31 AM	5:48 AM	10:57 AM	6:15 PM	6	6
SUN 20	1:46 AM	6:44 AM	11:35 AM	7:13 PM	7	7
MON 21	3:01 AM	7:43 AM	12:21 PM	8:14 PM	7	8
TUE 22	4:13 AM	8:46 AM	1:17 PM	9:17 PM	5	8
WED 23	5:18 AM	9:49 AM	2:23 PM	10:19 PM	6	7
THUR 24	6:11 AM	10:50 AM	3:35 PM	11:18 PM	8	8
FRI 25	6:54 AM	11:47 AM	4:47 PM		● 8	8
SAT 26	7:28 AM	12:39 PM	5:57 PM	12:13 AM	8	6
SUN 27	7:56 AM	1:26 PM	7:04 PM	1:02 AM	7	6
MON 28	8:20 AM	2:09 PM	8:07 PM	1:47 AM	6	7
TUE 29	8:43 AM	2:50 PM	9:08 PM	2:29 AM	5	5
WED 30	9:04 AM	3:31 PM	10:07 PM	3:10 AM	4	6
THUR 31	9:26 AM	4:11 PM	11:07 PM	3:51 AM	3	5

SOLAR/LUNAR BITE TIMES

Tim Smith's

Apogee moon phase on Saturday 2nd and Saturday 30th
Perigee moon phase on Friday 15th
● **New moon on Saturday 23rd**
First quarter moon on Friday 1st and Sunday 31st
○ **Full moon on Saturday 9th**
Last quarter moon phase on Saturday 16th

Brisbane, QLD: Rise: 06:10am Set: 05:20pm

(Note: These sun rise/set times are averages for the month)

DAY	MINOR BITE	MAJOR BITE	MINOR BITE	MAJOR BITE	SALT WATER RATING	FRESH WATER RATING
FRI 1	9:50 AM	4:53 PM		4:31 AM	4	6
SAT 2	10:17 AM	5:38 PM	12:07 AM	5:15 AM	4	6
SUN 3	10:49 AM	6:25 PM	1:09 AM	6:01 AM	5	6
MON 4	11:27 AM	7:16 PM	2:10 AM	6:50 AM	4	5
TUE 5	12:13 PM	8:09 PM	3:10 AM	7:42 AM	3	5
WED 6	1:08 PM	9:04 PM	4:06 AM	8:36 AM	6	6
THUR 7	2:11 PM	9:59 PM	4:55 AM	9:31 AM	5	7
FRI 8	3:19 PM	10:52 PM	5:38 AM	10:25 AM	3	8
SAT 9	4:29 PM	11:43 PM	6:14 AM	11:17 AM	○ 5	7
SUN 10	5:39 PM		6:45 AM	12:07 PM	7	6
MON 11	6:49 PM	12:32 AM	7:13 AM	12:55 PM	7	6

AUGUST 2025

POPULAR LOCATION ADJUSTMENTS (See full list on page 7)

DAY	MINOR BITE	MAJOR BITE	MINOR BITE	MAJOR BITE	SALT WATER RATING	FRESH WATER RATING
TUE 12	7:59 PM	1:19 AM	7:38 AM	1:43 PM	5	5
WED 13	9:09 PM	2:07 AM	8:03 AM	2:31 PM	4	4
THUR 14	10:22 PM	2:55 AM	8:30 AM	3:20 PM	3	6
FRI 15	11:36 PM	3:45 AM	8:59 AM	4:11 PM	4	4
SAT 16		4:39 AM	9:34 AM	5:07 PM	5	5
SUN 17	12:51 AM	5:36 AM	10:17 AM	6:06 PM	6	6
MON 18	2:03 AM	6:37 AM	11:09 AM	7:07 PM	7	7
TUE 19	3:09 AM	7:39 AM	12:10 PM	8:09 PM	7	8
WED 20	4:05 AM	8:40 AM	1:19 PM	9:08 PM	5	8
THUR 21	4:50 AM	9:37 AM	2:30 PM	10:03 PM	6	7
FRI 22	5:27 AM	10:30 AM	3:41 PM	10:53 PM	8	8
SAT 23	5:57 AM	11:18 AM	4:48 PM	11:40 PM	● 8	8
SUN 24	6:22 AM	12:03 PM	5:52 PM		8	6
MON 25	6:45 AM	12:45 PM	6:54 PM	12:24 AM	7	6
TUE 26	7:07 AM	1:26 PM	7:55 PM	1:05 AM	7	6
WED 27	7:28 AM	2:06 PM	8:55 PM	1:46 AM	6	7
THUR 28	7:51 AM	2:48 PM	9:55 PM	2:27 AM	5	5
FRI 29	8:17 AM	3:32 PM	10:56 PM	3:09 AM	4	6
SAT 30	8:47 AM	4:18 PM	11:57 PM	3:54 AM	3	5
SUN 31	9:22 AM	5:07 PM		4:42 AM	4	6

SOLAR/LUNAR BITE TIMES

Tim Smith's

Apogee moon phase on Friday 26th
Perigee moon phase on Wednesday 10th
● **New moon on Monday 22nd**
First quarter moon on Monday 29th
○ **Full moon on Monday 8th**
Last quarter moon phase on Sunday 14th

Brisbane, QLD: Rise: 05:40am Set: 05:40pm

(Note: These sun rise/set times are averages for the month)

DAY	MINOR BITE	MAJOR BITE	MINOR BITE	MAJOR BITE	SALT WATER RATING	FRESH WATER RATING
MON 1	10:05 AM	5:58 PM	12:57 AM	5:32 AM	5	6
TUE 2	10:55 AM	6:52 PM	1:55 AM	6:25 AM	4	5
WED 3	11:54 AM	7:46 PM	2:47 AM	7:18 AM	3	5
THUR 4	12:59 PM	8:40 PM	3:32 AM	8:13 AM	6	6
FRI 5	2:08 PM	9:32 PM	4:10 AM	9:05 AM	5	7
SAT 6	3:19 PM	10:22 PM	4:44 AM	9:56 AM	5	7
SUN 7	4:30 PM	11:11 PM	5:13 AM	10:46 AM	3	8
MON 8	5:42 PM	11:59 PM	5:39 AM	11:35 AM	○ 5	7
TUE 9	6:54 PM		6:05 AM	12:23 PM	7	6
WED 10	8:08 PM	12:48 AM	6:32 AM	1:13 PM	7	6
THUR 11	9:24 PM	1:39 AM	7:01 AM	2:05 PM	5	5

POPULAR LOCATION ADJUSTMENTS (See full list on page 7)

DAY	MINOR BITE	MAJOR BITE	MINOR BITE	MAJOR BITE	SALT WATER RATING	FRESH WATER RATING
FRI 12	10:40 PM	2:33 AM	7:34 AM	3:01 PM	3	6
SAT 13	11:55 PM	3:31 AM	8:15 AM	4:00 PM	4	4
SUN 14		4:31 AM	9:05 AM	5:02 PM	5	5
MON 15	1:03 AM	5:33 AM	10:03 AM	6:03 PM	6	6
TUE 16	2:02 AM	6:34 AM	11:10 AM	7:03 PM	7	7
WED 17	2:50 AM	7:32 AM	12:20 PM	7:58 PM	7	8
THUR 18	3:28 AM	8:25 AM	1:29 PM	8:49 PM	7	8
FRI 19	3:59 AM	9:14 AM	2:37 PM	9:36 PM	5	8
SAT 20	4:26 AM	9:59 AM	3:41 PM	10:19 PM	6	7
SUN 21	4:49 AM	10:41 AM	4:43 PM	11:01 PM	8	8
MON 22	5:11 AM	11:22 AM	5:44 PM	11:42 PM ●	8	8
TUE 23	5:32 AM	12:03 PM	6:44 PM		8	6
WED 24	5:55 AM	12:44 PM	7:44 PM	12:23 AM	7	6
THUR 25	6:19 AM	1:27 PM	8:45 PM	1:05 AM	6	7
FRI 26	6:47 AM	2:12 PM	9:46 PM	1:49 AM	5	5
SAT 27	7:20 AM	2:59 PM	10:46 PM	2:35 AM	4	6
SUN 28	7:59 AM	3:50 PM	11:44 PM	3:24 AM	4	6
MON 29	8:46 AM	4:42 PM		4:15 AM	3	5
TUE 30	9:40 AM	5:35 PM	12:38 AM	5:08 AM	4	6

SOLAR/LUNAR BITE TIMES

Tim Smith's

Apogee moon phase on Friday 24th
Perigee moon phase on Wednesday 8th
● **New moon on Tuesday 21st**
First quarter moon on Thursday 30th
○ **Full moon on Tuesday 7th**
Last quarter moon phase on Tuesday 14th

Brisbane, QLD: Rise: 05:10am Set: 05:50pm
(Note: These sun rise/set times are averages for the month)

DAY	MINOR BITE	MAJOR BITE	MINOR BITE	MAJOR BITE	SALT WATER RATING	FRESH WATER RATING
WED 1	10:42 AM	6:28 PM	1:24 AM	6:01 AM	5	6
THUR 2	11:48 AM	7:19 PM	2:05 AM	6:53 AM	4	5
FRI 3	12:57 PM	8:09 PM	2:40 AM	7:44 AM	3	5
SAT 4	2:07 PM	8:58 PM	3:10 AM	8:33 AM	6	6
SUN 5	3:17 PM	9:47 PM	3:38 AM	9:22 AM	5	7
MON 6	4:30 PM	10:36 PM	4:04 AM	10:11 AM	3	8
TUE 7	5:44 PM	11:27 PM	4:30 AM	11:01 AM	○ 5	7
WED 8	7:01 PM		4:59 AM	11:54 AM	7	6
THUR 9	8:21 PM	12:21 AM	5:31 AM	12:50 PM	7	6
FRI 10	9:39 PM	1:19 AM	6:10 AM	1:50 PM	5	5
SAT 11	10:53 PM	2:21 AM	6:58 AM	2:52 PM	4	4

DAY	MINOR BITE	MAJOR BITE	MINOR BITE	MAJOR BITE	SALT WATER RATING	FRESH WATER RATING
SUN 12	11:57 PM	3:25 AM	7:55 AM	3:56 PM	3	6
MON 13		4:28 AM	9:01 AM	4:57 PM	4	4
TUE 14	12:48 AM	5:27 AM	10:11 AM	5:54 PM	5	5
WED 15	1:30 AM	6:22 AM	11:21 AM	6:47 PM	6	6
THUR 16	2:03 AM	7:12 AM	12:29 PM	7:34 PM	7	7
FRI 17	2:30 AM	7:58 AM	1:34 PM	8:18 PM	7	8
SAT 18	2:54 AM	8:40 AM	2:35 PM	9:00 PM	5	8
SUN 19	3:16 AM	9:21 AM	3:36 PM	9:41 PM	6	7
MON 20	3:37 AM	10:01 AM	4:35 PM	10:21 PM	8	8
TUE 21	3:59 AM	10:42 AM	5:35 PM	11:03 PM ●	8	8
WED 22	4:23 AM	11:24 AM	6:35 PM	11:45 PM	8	8
THUR 23	4:49 AM	12:08 PM	7:36 PM		8	6
FRI 24	5:20 AM	12:55 PM	8:37 PM	12:31 AM	7	6
SAT 25	5:57 AM	1:44 PM	9:36 PM	1:19 AM	6	7
SUN 26	6:41 AM	2:35 PM	10:31 PM	2:09 AM	5	5
MON 27	7:32 AM	3:27 PM	11:19 PM	3:00 AM	4	6
TUE 28	8:30 AM	4:19 PM		3:53 AM	3	5
WED 29	9:33 AM	5:10 PM	12:01 AM	4:44 AM	3	5
THUR 30	10:39 AM	5:59 PM	12:37 AM	5:34 AM	4	6
FRI 31	11:46 AM	6:47 PM	1:08 AM	6:23 AM	5	6

SOLAR/LUNAR BITE TIMES

Apogee moon phase on Thursday 20th
Perigee moon phase on Thursday 6th
⬤ **New moon on Thursday 20th**
First quarter moon on Friday 28th
◯ **Full moon on Wednesday 5th**
Last quarter moon phase on Wednesday 12th

Brisbane, QLD: Rise: 04:40am Set: 06:10pm

(Note: These sun rise/set times are averages for the month)

DAY	MINOR BITE	MAJOR BITE	MINOR BITE	MAJOR BITE	SALT WATER RATING	FRESH WATER RATING
SAT 1	12:54 PM	7:34 PM	1:36 AM	7:10 AM	4	5
SUN 2	2:04 PM	8:21 PM	2:02 AM	7:57 AM	3	5
MON 3	3:16 PM	9:11 PM	2:28 AM	8:46 AM	6	6
TUE 4	4:31 PM	10:03 PM	2:55 AM	9:37 AM	3	8
WED 5	5:50 PM	11:00 PM	3:25 AM	10:31 AM	◯ 5	7
THUR 6	7:12 PM		4:01 AM	11:31 AM	7	6
FRI 7	8:31 PM	12:02 AM	4:46 AM	12:34 PM	7	6
SAT 8	9:42 PM	1:07 AM	5:41 AM	1:39 PM	5	5
SUN 9	10:41 PM	2:13 AM	6:46 AM	2:45 PM	4	4
MON 10	11:27 PM	3:17 AM	7:57 AM	3:46 PM	3	6
TUE 11		4:16 AM	9:10 AM	4:41 PM	4	4

DAY	MINOR BITE	MAJOR BITE	MINOR BITE	MAJOR BITE	SALT WATER RATING	FRESH WATER RATING
WED 12	12:04 AM	5:08 AM	10:20 AM	5:32 PM	5	5
THUR 13	12:33 AM	5:56 AM	11:27 AM	6:18 PM	6	6
FRI 14	12:59 AM	6:40 AM	12:29 PM	7:00 PM	7	7
SAT 15	1:21 AM	7:21 AM	1:30 PM	7:41 PM	7	7
SUN 16	1:42 AM	8:01 AM	2:29 PM	8:21 PM	7	8
MON 17	2:04 AM	8:41 AM	3:28 PM	9:01 PM	5	8
TUE 18	2:27 AM	9:22 AM	4:28 PM	9:44 PM	6	7
WED 19	2:53 AM	10:06 AM	5:29 PM	10:29 PM	8	8
THUR 20	3:22 AM	10:52 AM	6:30 PM	11:15 PM ●	8	8
FRI 21	3:57 AM	11:40 AM	7:29 PM		8	6
SAT 22	4:39 AM	12:31 PM	8:25 PM	12:05 AM	7	6
SUN 23	5:28 AM	1:23 PM	9:16 PM	12:57 AM	7	6
MON 24	6:24 AM	2:15 PM	10:00 PM	1:49 AM	6	7
TUE 25	7:25 AM	3:05 PM	10:37 PM	2:39 AM	5	5
WED 26	8:29 AM	3:54 PM	11:09 PM	3:29 AM	4	6
THUR 27	9:34 AM	4:41 PM	11:37 PM	4:17 AM	3	5
FRI 28	10:39 AM	5:26 PM		5:03 AM	4	6
SAT 29	11:46 AM	6:12 PM	12:02 AM	5:48 AM	5	6
SUN 30	12:54 PM	6:58 PM	12:27 AM	6:34 AM	4	5

SOLAR/LUNAR BITE TIMES

Tim Smith's

Apogee moon phase on **Wednesday 17th**
Perigee moon phase on **Thursday 4th**
⚫ **New moon on Satday 20th**
First quarter moon on **Sunday 28th**
◯ **Full moon on Friday 5th**
Last quarter moon phase on **Friday 12th**

Brisbane, QLD: Rise: 04:40am Set: 06:30pm
(Note: These sun rise/set times are averages for the month)

DAY	MINOR BITE	MAJOR BITE	MINOR BITE	MAJOR BITE	SALT WATER RATING	FRESH WATER RATING
MON 1	2:04 PM	7:47 PM	12:52 AM	7:22 AM	3	5
TUE 2	3:19 PM	8:40 PM	1:20 AM	8:13 AM	6	6
WED 3	4:38 PM	9:39 PM	1:52 AM	9:09 AM	5	7
THUR 4	5:59 PM	10:43 PM	2:31 AM	10:11 AM	3	8
FRI 5	7:16 PM	11:50 PM	3:21 AM	11:16 AM ◯	5	7
SAT 6	8:23 PM		4:22 AM	12:23 PM	7	6
SUN 7	9:17 PM	12:57 AM	5:33 AM	1:28 PM	7	6
MON 8	10:00 PM	2:00 AM	6:49 AM	2:28 PM	5	5
TUE 9	10:33 PM	2:58 AM	8:03 AM	3:23 PM	4	4
WED 10	11:01 PM	3:49 AM	9:13 AM	4:12 PM	3	6
THUR 11	11:25 PM	4:36 AM	10:19 AM	4:57 PM	4	4

DECEMBER 2025

POPULAR LOCATION ADJUSTMENTS (See full list on page 7)

DAY	MINOR BITE	MAJOR BITE	MINOR BITE	MAJOR BITE	SALT WATER RATING	FRESH WATER RATING
FRI 12	11:47 PM	5:19 AM	11:22 AM	5:39 PM	5	5
SAT 13		6:00 AM	12:22 PM	6:19 PM	6	6
SUN 14	12:08 AM	6:40 AM	1:21 PM	7:00 PM	7	7
MON 15	12:31 AM	7:21 AM	2:21 PM	7:42 PM	7	8
TUE 16	12:56 AM	8:04 AM	3:21 PM	8:26 PM	5	8
WED 17	1:24 AM	8:49 AM	4:22 PM	9:12 PM	5	8
THUR 18	1:57 AM	9:36 AM	5:22 PM	10:01 PM	6	7
FRI 19	2:37 AM	10:27 AM	6:20 PM	10:52 PM	8	8
SAT 20	3:24 AM	11:19 AM	7:13 PM	11:45 PM	● 8	8
SUN 21	4:19 AM	12:11 PM	7:59 PM		8	6
MON 22	5:19 AM	1:02 PM	8:38 PM	12:36 AM	7	6
TUE 23	6:22 AM	1:52 PM	9:11 PM	1:26 AM	6	7
WED 24	7:27 AM	2:39 PM	9:40 PM	2:15 AM	5	5
THUR 25	8:32 AM	3:24 PM	10:06 PM	3:01 AM	4	6
FRI 26	9:37 AM	4:09 PM	10:30 PM	3:46 AM	4	6
SAT 27	10:42 AM	4:53 PM	10:54 PM	4:30 AM	3	5
SUN 28	11:49 AM	5:39 PM	11:19 PM	5:15 AM	4	6
MON 29	12:59 PM	6:28 PM	11:48 PM	6:03 AM	5	6
TUE 30	2:14 PM	7:22 PM		6:55 AM	4	5
WED 31	3:31 PM	8:21 PM	12:23 AM	7:51 AM	3	5

TIDE TIMES

Tim Smith's

Townsville

POPULAR TIDE ADJUSTMENTS

Abbot Point	+40min
Cairns	+ 5min
Lucinda	0
Mackay Outer Harbour	+2hr 25min
Mourilyan Low tide	-15min
Mourilyan High tide	+5min
Port Douglas Low Tide	-20min
Port Douglas High Tide	0
Shute Harbour	+ 2hr 5min
Bowen	+ 35min
Cooktown	0
Flinders Reef	- 20min

Day	Date		Tide 1	
Sun	1		2:54 AM	(0.97) L
Mon	2		3:14 AM	(1.04) L
Tue	3	●	3:28 AM	(1.11) L
Wed	4		3:37 AM	(1.16) L
THu	5		3:45 AM	(1.20) L
Fri	6		3:55 AM	(1.24) L
Sat	7		4:06 AM	(1.30) L
Sun	8		4:22 AM	(1.37) L
Mon	9		4:40 AM	(1.47) L
Tue	10		5:06 AM	(1.60) L
Wed	11		12:38 AM	(1.70) L
THu	12		12:31 AM	(1.49) L
Fri	13		12:48 AM	(1.29) L
Sat	14		1:12 AM	(1.10) L
Sun	15		1:38 AM	(0.91) L
Mon	16		2:05 AM	(0.73) L
Tue	17		2:33 AM	(0.59) L
Wed	18	○	3:03 AM	(0.50) L
THu	19		3:35 AM	(0.50) L
Fri	20		4:11 AM	(0.60) L
Sat	21		4:52 AM	(0.78) L
Sun	22		5:55 AM	(1.03) L
Mon	23		7:31 AM	(1.23) L
Tue	24		3:20 AM	(1.85) H
Wed	25		5:23 AM	(2.07) H
THu	26		12:29 AM	(1.02) L
Fri	27		1:03 AM	(0.88) L
Sat	28		1:33 AM	(0.84) L
Sun	29		1:59 AM	(0.86) L
Mon	30		2:19 AM	(0.91) L

SEPTEMBER 2024

Tide 2		Tide 3		Tide 4	
8:10 AM	(2.64) H	2:20 PM	(0.67) L	8:36 PM	(3.44) H
8:32 AM	(2.66) H	2:37 PM	(0.74) L	9:00 PM	(3.36) H
8:55 AM	(2.65) H	2:53 PM	(0.85) L	9:24 PM	(3.24) H
9:17 AM	(2.61) H	3:09 PM	(1.00) L	9:45 PM	(3.08) H
9:43 AM	(2.54) H	3:25 PM	(1.20) L	10:04 PM	(2.88) H
10:12 AM	(2.45) H	3:39 PM	(1.43) L	10:17 PM	(2.65) H
10:49 AM	(2.34) H	3:50 PM	(1.67) L	10:25 PM	(2.42) H
11:44 AM	(2.22) H	3:54 PM	(1.91) L	10:18 PM	(2.20) H
1:22 PM	(2.15) H	3:16 PM	(2.13) L	6:03 PM	(2.20) H
6:08 AM	(1.61) H	8:01 AM	(1.57) L	5:55 PM	(2.42) H
4:21 AM	(1.76) H	9:59 AM	(1.46) L	5:56 PM	(2.66) H
5:20 AM	(1.96) H	11:02 AM	(1.25) L	6:11 PM	(2.92) H
5:46 AM	(2.19) H	11:45 AM	(0.99) L	6:33 PM	(3.18) H
6:14 AM	(2.45) H	12:20 PM	(0.73) L	6:59 PM	(3.45) H
6:44 AM	(2.73) H	12:54 PM	(0.48) L	7:27 PM	(3.68) H
7:18 AM	(2.99) H	1:29 PM	(0.31) L	7:58 PM	(3.85) H
7:57 AM	(3.20) H	2:04 PM	(0.25) L	8:30 PM	(3.90) H
8:40 AM	(3.32) H	2:43 PM	(0.35) L	9:06 PM	(3.80) H
9:26 AM	(3.32) H	3:25 PM	(0.60) L	9:43 PM	(3.53) H
10:16 AM	(3.22) H	4:16 PM	(0.99) L	10:20 PM	(3.13) H
11:13 AM	(3.03) H	5:38 PM	(1.42) L	11:00 PM	(2.64) H
12:25 PM	(2.81) H	7:33 PM	(1.71) L	11:53 PM	(2.15) H
2:41 PM	(2.73) H	10:23 PM	(1.61) L		
9:29 AM	(1.25) L	4:43 PM	(2.95) H	11:45 PM	(1.27) L
10:53 AM	(1.10) L	5:41 PM	(3.18) H		
6:06 AM	(2.30) H	11:51 AM	(0.93) L	6:19 PM	(3.31) H
6:37 AM	(2.48) H	12:35 PM	(0.82) L	6:49 PM	(3.36) H
7:03 AM	(2.61) H	1:10 PM	(0.78) L	7:15 PM	(3.36) H
7:27 AM	(2.70) H	1:36 PM	(0.80) L	7:38 PM	(3.33) H
7:48 AM	(2.76) H	1:56 PM	(0.87) L	8:00 PM	(3.27) H

TIDE TIMES

Tim Smith's

POPULAR TIDE ADJUSTMENTS

Abbot Point	+40min
Cairns	+ 5min
Lucinda	0
Mackay Outer Harbour	+2hr 25min
Mourilyan Low tide	-15min
Mourilyan High tide	+5min
Port Douglas Low Tide	-20min
Port Douglas High Tide	0
Shute Harbour	+ 2hr 5min
Bowen	+ 35min
Cooktown	0
Flinders Reef	- 20min

Townsville

Day	Date		Tide 1	
Tue	1		2:32 AM	(0.95) L
Wed	2		2:39 AM	(0.97) L
THu	3 ●		2:44 AM	(0.97) L
Fri	4		2:52 AM	(0.97) L
Sat	5		3:05 AM	(0.99) L
Sun	6		3:21 AM	(1.05) L
Mon	7		3:38 AM	(1.15) L
Tue	8		3:57 AM	(1.30) L
Wed	9		4:20 AM	(1.49) L
THu	10		4:27 AM	(1.72) H
Fri	11		5:00 AM	(1.98) H
Sat	12		12:14 AM	(1.14) L
Sun	13		12:39 AM	(0.93) L
Mon	14		1:05 AM	(0.73) L
Tue	15		1:33 AM	(0.54) L
Wed	16		2:00 AM	(0.39) L
THu	17 ○		2:30 AM	(0.31) L
Fri	18		3:00 AM	(0.33) L
Sat	19		3:33 AM	(0.46) L
Sun	20		4:12 AM	(0.69) L
Mon	21		5:09 AM	(0.99) L
Tue	22		6:51 AM	(1.26) L
Wed	23		3:17 AM	(1.80) H
THu	24		4:57 AM	(2.06) H
Fri	25		5:40 AM	(2.30) H
Sat	26		12:31 AM	(0.90) L
Sun	27		1:00 AM	(0.86) L
Mon	28		1:24 AM	(0.86) L
Tue	29		1:42 AM	(0.87) L
Wed	30		1:52 AM	(0.87) L
THu	31		1:59 AM	(0.85) L

Tide 2	Tide 3	Tide 4
8:10 AM (2.79) **H**	2:12 PM (0.95) L	8:20 PM (3.18) **H**
8:31 AM (2.80) **H**	2:27 PM (1.07) L	8:38 PM (3.05) **H**
8:54 AM (2.79) **H**	2:44 PM (1.21) L	8:53 PM (2.89) **H**
9:19 AM (2.75) **H**	3:00 PM (1.38) L	9:06 PM (2.71) **H**
9:48 AM (2.69) **H**	3:16 PM (1.58) L	9:17 PM (2.52) **H**
10:25 AM (2.60) **H**	3:32 PM (1.78) L	9:29 PM (2.31) **H**
11:15 AM (2.48) **H**	3:48 PM (2.00) L	9:26 PM (2.09) **H**
12:34 PM (2.37) **H**	4:01 PM (2.23) L	5:03 PM (2.24) **H**
4:46 PM (2.48) **H**	11:52 PM (1.58) L	
9:02 AM (1.51) L	5:03 PM (2.74) **H**	11:53 PM (1.36) L
10:28 AM (1.30) L	5:29 PM (3.00) **H**	
5:28 AM (2.27) **H**	11:16 AM (1.04) L	5:55 PM (3.26) **H**
5:57 AM (2.57) **H**	11:57 AM (0.80) L	6:23 PM (3.48) **H**
6:29 AM (2.88) **H**	12:33 PM (0.62) L	6:51 PM (3.66) **H**
7:04 AM (3.17) **H**	1:10 PM (0.51) L	7:22 PM (3.74) **H**
7:44 AM (3.40) **H**	1:49 PM (0.53) L	7:56 PM (3.69) **H**
8:27 AM (3.53) **H**	2:33 PM (0.67) L	8:30 PM (3.50) **H**
9:14 AM (3.54) **H**	3:26 PM (0.93) L	9:08 PM (3.18) **H**
10:05 AM (3.43) **H**	4:34 PM (1.26) L	9:47 PM (2.76) **H**
11:01 AM (3.24) **H**	5:59 PM (1.54) L	10:32 PM (2.32) **H**
12:12 PM (3.01) **H**	7:54 PM (1.64) L	11:43 PM (1.91) **H**
2:09 PM (2.89) **H**	10:05 PM (1.45) L	
8:56 AM (1.33) L	4:00 PM (2.98) **H**	11:15 PM (1.19) L
10:20 AM (1.24) L	5:01 PM (3.10) **H**	11:57 PM (1.00) L
11:21 AM (1.13) L	5:42 PM (3.17) **H**	
6:13 AM (2.49) **H**	12:07 PM (1.06) L	6:13 PM (3.19) **H**
6:41 AM (2.63) **H**	12:44 PM (1.05) L	6:38 PM (3.17) **H**
7:06 AM (2.73) **H**	1:13 PM (1.09) L	7:00 PM (3.12) **H**
7:30 AM (2.81) **H**	1:37 PM (1.15) L	7:20 PM (3.04) **H**
7:54 AM (2.88) **H**	1:58 PM (1.24) L	7:37 PM (2.94) **H**
8:16 AM (2.92) **H**	2:19 PM (1.33) L	7:53 PM (2.83) **H**

TIDE TIMES

Tam Smith's

Townsville

POPULAR TIDE ADJUSTMENTS

Abbot Point	+40min
Cairns	+ 5min
Lucinda	0
Mackay Outer Harbour	+2hr 25min
Mourilyan Low tide	-15min
Mourilyan High tide	+5min
Port Douglas Low Tide	-20min
Port Douglas High Tide	0
Shute Harbour	+ 2hr 5min
Bowen	+ 35min
Cooktown	0
Flinders Reef	- 20min

Day	Date	Tide 1	
Fri	1 ●	2:06 AM	(0.82) L
Sat	2	2:19 AM	(0.80) L
Sun	3	2:37 AM	(0.82) L
Mon	4	3:00 AM	(0.89) L
Tue	5	3:26 AM	(1.02) L
Wed	6	4:00 AM	(1.20) L
THu	7	5:18 AM	(1.40) L
Fri	8	2:47 AM	(1.77) H
Sat	9	4:13 AM	(2.03) H
Sun	10	4:58 AM	(2.34) H
Mon	11	12:04 AM	(0.85) L
Tue	12	12:34 AM	(0.64) L
Wed	13	1:04 AM	(0.46) L
THu	14	1:33 AM	(0.33) L
Fri	15	2:04 AM	(0.27) L
Sat	16 ○	2:37 AM	(0.30) L
Sun	17	3:14 AM	(0.44) L
Mon	18	3:56 AM	(0.66) L
Tue	19	4:49 AM	(0.93) L
Wed	20	6:04 AM	(1.20) L
THu	21	2:09 AM	(1.83) H
Fri	22	3:56 AM	(1.98) H
Sat	23	5:02 AM	(2.20) H
Sun	24	5:46 AM	(2.40) H
Mon	25	12:26 AM	(0.99) L
Tue	26	12:49 AM	(0.94) L
Wed	27	1:07 AM	(0.91) L
THu	28	1:19 AM	(0.87) L
Fri	29	1:30 AM	(0.82) L
Sat	30	1:43 AM	(0.76) L

Tide 2		Tide 3		Tide 4	
8:41 AM	(2.95) H	2:43 PM	(1.44) L	8:08 PM	(2.70) H
9:08 AM	(2.96) H	3:09 PM	(1.56) L	8:26 PM	(2.56) H
9:40 AM	(2.93) H	3:49 PM	(1.70) L	8:48 PM	(2.40) H
10:20 AM	(2.85) H	5:15 PM	(1.83) L	9:15 PM	(2.21) H
11:11 AM	(2.75) H	6:48 PM	(1.89) L	9:45 PM	(2.00) H
12:18 PM	(2.66) H	9:34 PM	(1.77) L	10:55 PM	(1.78) H
2:04 PM	(2.66) H	10:30 PM	(1.54) L		
8:04 AM	(1.46) L	3:45 PM	(2.84) H	11:02 PM	(1.31) L
9:40 AM	(1.35) L	4:34 PM	(3.05) H	11:33 PM	(1.07) L
10:43 AM	(1.18) L	5:12 PM	(3.24) H		
5:37 AM	(2.66) H	11:32 AM	(1.03) L	5:45 PM	(3.37) H
6:15 AM	(2.97) H	12:18 PM	(0.93) L	6:16 PM	(3.44) H
6:55 AM	(3.27) H	1:03 PM	(0.89) L	6:50 PM	(3.42) H
7:36 AM	(3.50) H	1:51 PM	(0.92) L	7:26 PM	(3.31) H
8:21 AM	(3.64) H	2:45 PM	(1.03) L	8:05 PM	(3.10) H
9:09 AM	(3.67) H	3:43 PM	(1.19) L	8:46 PM	(2.82) H
9:59 AM	(3.60) H	4:48 PM	(1.36) L	9:31 PM	(2.50) H
10:53 AM	(3.43) H	6:02 PM	(1.50) L	10:26 PM	(2.18) H
11:54 AM	(3.22) H	7:33 PM	(1.54) L	11:42 PM	(1.92) H
1:12 PM	(3.03) H	9:06 PM	(1.45) L		
7:55 AM	(1.39) L	2:45 PM	(2.95) H	10:25 PM	(1.30) L
9:28 AM	(1.44) L	4:00 PM	(2.94) H	11:17 PM	(1.16) L
10:37 AM	(1.43) L	4:51 PM	(2.95) H	11:56 PM	(1.06) L
11:32 AM	(1.41) L	5:29 PM	(2.94) H		
6:21 AM	(2.57) H	12:17 PM	(1.41) L	5:58 PM	(2.91) H
6:51 AM	(2.72) H	12:55 PM	(1.42) L	6:22 PM	(2.85) H
7:18 AM	(2.84) H	1:27 PM	(1.45) L	6:42 PM	(2.78) H
7:44 AM	(2.95) H	1:57 PM	(1.48) L	7:00 PM	(2.70) H
8:08 AM	(3.04) H	2:27 PM	(1.52) L	7:19 PM	(2.64) H
8:33 AM	(3.12) H	2:59 PM	(1.55) L	7:43 PM	(2.57) H

TIDE TIMES

Tim Smith's

POPULAR TIDE ADJUSTMENTS

Abbot Point	+40min
Cairns	+ 5min
Lucinda	0
Mackay Outer Harbour	+2hr 25min
Mourilyan Low tide	-15min
Mourilyan High tide	+5min
Port Douglas Low Tide	-20min
Port Douglas High Tide	0
Shute Harbour	+ 2hr 5min
Bowen	+ 35min
Cooktown	0
Flinders Reef	- 20min

Townsville

Day	Date		Tide 1	
Sun	1	●	2:02 AM	(0.72) L
Mon	2		2:29 AM	(0.72) L
Tue	3		3:00 AM	(0.77) L
Wed	4		3:38 AM	(0.88) L
THu	5		4:26 AM	(1.03) L
Fri	6		5:32 AM	(1.21) L
Sat	7		1:25 AM	(1.97) H
Sun	8		3:15 AM	(2.12) H
Mon	9		4:27 AM	(2.39) H
Tue	10		5:22 AM	(2.71) H
Wed	11		12:09 AM	(0.69) L
THu	12		12:45 AM	(0.53) L
Fri	13		1:18 AM	(0.42) L
Sat	14		1:54 AM	(0.36) L
Sun	15	○	2:30 AM	(0.38) L
Mon	16		3:09 AM	(0.47) L
Tue	17		3:49 AM	(0.63) L
Wed	18		4:30 AM	(0.85) L
THu	19		5:15 AM	(1.10) L
Fri	20		12:22 AM	(2.01) H
Sat	21		2:14 AM	(1.95) H
Sun	22		4:07 AM	(2.06) H
Mon	23		5:30 AM	(2.27) H
Tue	24		6:15 AM	(2.50) H
Wed	25		12:16 AM	(1.13) L
THu	26		12:36 AM	(1.05) L
Fri	27		12:54 AM	(0.97) L
Sat	28		1:12 AM	(0.87) L
Sun	29		1:32 AM	(0.77) L
Mon	30		1:58 AM	(0.68) L
Tue	31	●	2:29 AM	(0.61) L

Tide 2		Tide 3		Tide 4	
9:03 AM	(3.17) H	3:35 PM	(1.59) L	8:11 PM	(2.49) H
9:37 AM	(3.18) H	4:20 PM	(1.64) L	8:45 PM	(2.40) H
10:18 AM	(3.15) H	5:15 PM	(1.69) L	9:26 PM	(2.27) H
11:05 AM	(3.09) H	6:22 PM	(1.72) L	10:21 PM	(2.13) H
12:00 PM	(3.03) H	7:44 PM	(1.67) L	11:45 PM	(2.00) H
1:05 PM	(2.98) H	9:01 PM	(1.53) L		
7:06 AM	(1.36) L	2:21 PM	(2.98) H	10:01 PM	(1.33) L
8:45 AM	(1.43) L	3:31 PM	(3.03) H	10:49 PM	(1.11) L
10:09 AM	(1.42) L	4:25 PM	(3.08) H	11:31 PM	(0.89) L
11:18 AM	(1.37) L	5:10 PM	(3.10) H		
6:10 AM	(3.03) H	12:21 PM	(1.31) L	5:51 PM	(3.07) H
6:55 AM	(3.32) H	1:17 PM	(1.25) L	6:31 PM	(3.01) H
7:39 AM	(3.56) H	2:10 PM	(1.22) L	7:14 PM	(2.92) H
8:23 AM	(3.71) H	3:01 PM	(1.22) L	7:58 PM	(2.79) H
9:07 AM	(3.77) H	3:52 PM	(1.25) L	8:44 PM	(2.64) H
9:53 AM	(3.73) H	4:45 PM	(1.33) L	9:31 PM	(2.48) H
10:39 AM	(3.59) H	5:42 PM	(1.42) L	10:20 PM	(2.31) H
11:26 AM	(3.40) H	6:45 PM	(1.52) L	11:15 PM	(2.15) H
12:16 PM	(3.18) H	7:56 PM	(1.57) L		
6:07 AM	(1.37) L	1:13 PM	(2.97) H	9:11 PM	(1.54) L
7:37 AM	(1.62) L	2:19 PM	(2.80) H	10:23 PM	(1.45) L
9:32 AM	(1.76) L	3:30 PM	(2.70) H	11:15 PM	(1.34) L
10:57 AM	(1.79) L	4:30 PM	(2.65) H	11:50 PM	(1.23) L
12:00 PM	(1.75) L	5:14 PM	(2.60) H		
6:45 AM	(2.70) H	12:48 PM	(1.70) L	5:47 PM	(2.57) H
7:12 AM	(2.88) H	1:26 PM	(1.64) L	6:15 PM	(2.54) H
7:36 AM	(3.03) H	1:59 PM	(1.60) L	6:39 PM	(2.53) H
8:00 AM	(3.17) H	2:29 PM	(1.55) L	7:04 PM	(2.54) H
8:26 AM	(3.29) H	3:00 PM	(1.51) L	7:34 PM	(2.57) H
8:56 AM	(3.40) H	3:32 PM	(1.48) L	8:09 PM	(2.60) H
9:30 AM	(3.47) H	4:10 PM	(1.47) L	8:48 PM	(2.61) H

TIDE TIMES

Tim Smith's

Townsville

POPULAR TIDE ADJUSTMENTS

Abbot Point	+40min
Cairns	+ 5min
Lucinda	0
Mackay Outer Harbour	+2hr 25min
Mourilyan Low tide	-15min
Mourilyan High tide	+5min
Port Douglas Low Tide	-20min
Port Douglas High Tide	0
Shute Harbour	+ 2hr 5min
Bowen	+ 35min
Cooktown	0
Flinders Reef	- 20min

Day	Date	Tide 1	
Wed	1	3:04 AM	(0.61) L
THu	2	3:42 AM	(0.67) L
Fri	3	4:24 AM	(0.81) L
Sat	4	5:13 AM	(1.04) L
Sun	5	12:39 AM	(2.31) H
Mon	6	2:13 AM	(2.30) H
Tue	7	4:02 AM	(2.48) H
Wed	8	5:20 AM	(2.80) H
THu	9	6:17 AM	(3.13) H
Fri	10	12:38 AM	(0.71) L
Sat	11	1:17 AM	(0.59) L
Sun	12	1:55 AM	(0.51) L
Mon	13	2:30 AM	(0.48) L
Tue	14 ○	3:03 AM	(0.52) L
Wed	15	3:35 AM	(0.63) L
THu	16	4:03 AM	(0.81) L
Fri	17	4:28 AM	(1.06) L
Sat	18	4:50 AM	(1.34) L
Sun	19	12:04 AM	(2.16) H
Mon	20	1:40 AM	(2.05) H
Tue	21	6:30 AM	(2.24) H
Wed	22	6:32 AM	(2.50) H
THu	23	6:46 AM	(2.73) H
Fri	24	12:10 AM	(1.28) L
Sat	25	12:34 AM	(1.14) L
Sun	26	12:59 AM	(0.98) L
Mon	27	1:24 AM	(0.80) L
Tue	28	1:52 AM	(0.63) L
Wed	29 ●	2:23 AM	(0.50) L
THu	30	2:56 AM	(0.45) L
Fri	31	3:31 AM	(0.51) L

Tide 2		Tide 3		Tide 4	
10:07 AM	(3.51) **H**	4:53 PM	(1.49) L	9:34 PM	(2.58) **H**
10:48 AM	(3.49) **H**	5:43 PM	(1.51) L	10:27 PM	(2.50) **H**
11:33 AM	(3.41) **H**	6:41 PM	(1.52) L	11:28 PM	(2.40) **H**
12:21 PM	(3.28) **H**	7:46 PM	(1.49) L		
6:16 AM	(1.32) L	1:15 PM	(3.11) **H**	8:57 PM	(1.39) L
7:56 AM	(1.59) L	2:23 PM	(2.93) **H**	10:03 PM	(1.23) L
9:51 AM	(1.73) L	3:42 PM	(2.80) **H**	11:02 PM	(1.05) L
11:33 AM	(1.68) L	4:53 PM	(2.73) **H**	11:53 PM	(0.87) L
12:45 PM	(1.53) L	5:51 PM	(2.70) **H**		
7:04 AM	(3.42) **H**	1:39 PM	(1.38) L	6:41 PM	(2.70) **H**
7:45 AM	(3.65) **H**	2:25 PM	(1.27) L	7:25 PM	(2.72) **H**
8:23 AM	(3.79) **H**	3:07 PM	(1.21) L	8:07 PM	(2.74) **H**
9:00 AM	(3.85) **H**	3:45 PM	(1.22) L	8:46 PM	(2.73) **H**
9:38 AM	(3.81) **H**	4:24 PM	(1.28) L	9:24 PM	(2.69) **H**
10:15 AM	(3.69) **H**	5:01 PM	(1.39) L	10:00 PM	(2.60) **H**
10:51 AM	(3.51) **H**	5:41 PM	(1.52) L	10:35 PM	(2.47) **H**
11:26 AM	(3.28) **H**	6:24 PM	(1.65) L	11:14 PM	(2.32) **H**
12:01 PM	(3.03) **H**	7:20 PM	(1.73) L		
5:08 AM	(1.64) L	12:40 PM	(2.78) **H**	8:40 PM	(1.75) L
5:12 AM	(1.94) L	1:30 PM	(2.54) **H**	10:06 PM	(1.68) L
10:30 AM	(2.10) L	2:52 PM	(2.37) **H**	11:06 PM	(1.55) L
12:07 PM	(1.98) L	4:28 PM	(2.30) **H**	11:42 PM	(1.42) L
12:53 PM	(1.83) L	5:30 PM	(2.32) **H**		
7:04 AM	(2.93) **H**	1:25 PM	(1.69) L	6:07 PM	(2.37) **H**
7:24 AM	(3.12) **H**	1:52 PM	(1.58) L	6:34 PM	(2.46) **H**
7:45 AM	(3.30) **H**	2:17 PM	(1.48) L	7:01 PM	(2.59) **H**
8:11 AM	(3.48) **H**	2:45 PM	(1.39) L	7:31 PM	(2.73) **H**
8:39 AM	(3.65) **H**	3:14 PM	(1.31) L	8:06 PM	(2.87) **H**
9:10 AM	(3.78) **H**	3:45 PM	(1.25) L	8:45 PM	(2.97) **H**
9:45 AM	(3.84) **H**	4:20 PM	(1.23) L	9:29 PM	(3.00) **H**
10:21 AM	(3.81) **H**	5:00 PM	(1.24) L	10:15 PM	(2.95) **H**

TIDE TIMES

Tim Smith's

POPULAR TIDE ADJUSTMENTS

Abbot Point	+40min
Cairns	+ 5min
Lucinda	0
Mackay Outer Harbour	+2hr 25min
Mourilyan Low tide	-15min
Mourilyan High tide	+5min
Port Douglas Low Tide	-20min
Port Douglas High Tide	0
Shute Harbour	+ 2hr 5min
Bowen	+ 35min
Cooktown	0
Flinders Reef	- 20min

Townsville

Day	Date	Tide 1	
Sat	1	4:09 AM	(0.70) L
Sun	2	4:50 AM	(1.02) L
Mon	3	12:07 AM	(2.68) H
Tue	4	1:29 AM	(2.55) H
Wed	5	3:53 AM	(2.63) H
THu	6	5:32 AM	(2.96) H
Fri	7	6:28 AM	(3.30) H
Sat	8	12:39 AM	(0.87) L
Sun	9	1:20 AM	(0.72) L
Mon	10	1:55 AM	(0.63) L
Tue	11	2:25 AM	(0.59) L
Wed	12	2:49 AM	(0.63) L
THu	13 ○	3:12 AM	(0.73) L
Fri	14	3:31 AM	(0.90) L
Sat	15	3:48 AM	(1.13) L
Sun	16	4:03 AM	(1.40) L
Mon	17	4:15 AM	(1.68) L
Tue	18	4:15 AM	(1.96) L
Wed	19	1:26 AM	(2.20) H
THu	20	6:34 AM	(2.54) H
Fri	21	6:34 AM	(2.76) H
Sat	22	6:44 AM	(2.97) H
Sun	23	12:13 AM	(1.30) L
Mon	24	12:41 AM	(1.07) L
Tue	25	1:09 AM	(0.82) L
Wed	26	1:37 AM	(0.61) L
THu	27	2:07 AM	(0.45) L
Fri	28 ●	2:40 AM	(0.42) L

FEBRUARY 2025

Tide 2		Tide 3		Tide 4	
11:00 AM (3.66) **H**		5:45 PM (1.29) L		11:07 PM (2.83) **H**	
11:40 AM (3.40) **H**		6:41 PM (1.36) L			
5:45 AM (1.42) L		12:25 PM (3.07) **H**		7:51 PM (1.41) L	
7:38 AM (1.81) L		1:24 PM (2.70) **H**		9:16 PM (1.39) L	
10:20 AM (1.93) L		3:18 PM (2.43) **H**		10:42 PM (1.25) L	
12:07 PM (1.71) L		5:19 PM (2.42) **H**		11:48 PM (1.06) L	
1:05 PM (1.45) L		6:23 PM (2.53) **H**			
7:08 AM (3.55) **H**		1:48 PM (1.26) L		7:04 PM (2.65) **H**	
7:42 AM (3.72) **H**		2:25 PM (1.16) L		7:38 PM (2.77) **H**	
8:13 AM (3.81) **H**		2:56 PM (1.13) L		8:08 PM (2.87) **H**	
8:44 AM (3.83) **H**		3:25 PM (1.16) L		8:38 PM (2.93) **H**	
9:14 AM (3.78) **H**		3:50 PM (1.23) L		9:06 PM (2.93) **H**	
9:43 AM (3.67) **H**		4:12 PM (1.33) L		9:34 PM (2.87) **H**	
10:11 AM (3.49) **H**		4:29 PM (1.42) L		10:00 PM (2.77) **H**	
10:36 AM (3.26) **H**		4:44 PM (1.52) L		10:29 PM (2.64) **H**	
11:00 AM (3.01) **H**		4:56 PM (1.61) L		11:01 PM (2.48) **H**	
11:21 AM (2.74) **H**		5:10 PM (1.70) L		11:46 PM (2.32) **H**	
11:35 AM (2.47) **H**		5:31 PM (1.79) L			
3:07 AM (2.19) L		6:51 AM (2.31) **H**		8:40 PM (1.83) L	
12:47 PM (1.99) L		3:36 PM (2.03) **H**		10:55 PM (1.70) L	
12:55 PM (1.80) L		5:45 PM (2.15) **H**		11:41 PM (1.51) L	
1:12 PM (1.63) L		6:09 PM (2.30) **H**			
7:00 AM (3.18) **H**		1:31 PM (1.48) L		6:30 PM (2.49) **H**	
7:20 AM (3.41) **H**		1:54 PM (1.34) L		6:54 PM (2.72) **H**	
7:44 AM (3.63) **H**		2:19 PM (1.20) L		7:22 PM (2.95) **H**	
8:11 AM (3.84) **H**		2:45 PM (1.07) L		7:56 PM (3.17) **H**	
8:41 AM (3.98) **H**		3:13 PM (0.97) L		8:33 PM (3.33) **H**	
9:13 AM (4.01) **H**		3:43 PM (0.91) L		9:15 PM (3.40) **H**	

TIDE TIMES

Tim Smith's

Townsville

POPULAR TIDE ADJUSTMENTS

Abbot Point	+40min
Cairns	+ 5min
Lucinda	0
Mackay Outer Harbour	+2hr 25min
Mourilyan Low tide	-15min
Mourilyan High tide	+5min
Port Douglas Low Tide	-20min
Port Douglas High Tide	0
Shute Harbour	+ 2hr 5min
Bowen	+ 35min
Cooktown	0
Flinders Reef	- 20min

Day	Date	Tide 1	
Sat	1	3:15 AM	(0.53) L
Sun	2	3:52 AM	(0.79) L
Mon	3	4:36 AM	(1.18) L
Tue	4	5:48 AM	(1.64) L
Wed	5	1:05 AM	(2.80) H
THu	6	3:51 AM	(2.83) H
Fri	7	5:31 AM	(3.15) H
Sat	8	6:19 AM	(3.43) H
Sun	9	12:33 AM	(0.99) L
Mon	10	1:14 AM	(0.85) L
Tue	11	1:45 AM	(0.78) L
Wed	12	2:10 AM	(0.79) L
THu	13	2:30 AM	(0.85) L
Fri	14 ○	2:46 AM	(0.97) L
Sat	15	3:03 AM	(1.13) L
Sun	16	3:19 AM	(1.33) L
Mon	17	3:33 AM	(1.56) L
Tue	18	3:45 AM	(1.80) L
Wed	19	3:54 AM	(2.03) L
THu	20	12:04 AM	(2.46) H
Fri	21	5:58 AM	(2.53) H
Sat	22	5:57 AM	(2.75) H
Sun	23	6:05 AM	(2.97) H
Mon	24	6:22 AM	(3.21) H
Tue	25	12:13 AM	(1.15) L
Wed	26	12:44 AM	(0.89) L
THu	27	1:15 AM	(0.69) L
Fri	28	1:47 AM	(0.57) L
Sat	29 ●	2:23 AM	(0.58) L
Sun	30	3:01 AM	(0.74) L
Mon	31	3:47 AM	(1.04) L

Tide 2		Tide 3		Tide 4	
9:47 AM	(3.91) **H**	4:15 PM	(0.92) L	10:00 PM	(3.36) **H**
10:23 AM	(3.66) **H**	4:52 PM	(1.01) L	10:50 PM	(3.23) **H**
11:00 AM	(3.29) **H**	5:38 PM	(1.17) L	11:46 PM	(3.02) **H**
11:43 AM	(2.84) **H**	6:47 PM	(1.36) L		
8:11 AM	(1.97) L	12:44 PM	(2.38) **H**	8:31 PM	(1.49) L
11:06 AM	(1.83) L	4:08 PM	(2.15) **H**	10:27 PM	(1.40) L
12:18 PM	(1.49) L	5:51 PM	(2.36) **H**	11:42 PM	(1.19) L
1:01 PM	(1.25) L	6:34 PM	(2.57) **H**		
6:55 AM	(3.60) **H**	1:36 PM	(1.10) L	7:06 PM	(2.75) **H**
7:24 AM	(3.69) **H**	2:07 PM	(1.05) L	7:31 PM	(2.89) **H**
7:50 AM	(3.72) **H**	2:33 PM	(1.07) L	7:57 PM	(3.00) **H**
8:16 AM	(3.69) **H**	2:54 PM	(1.11) L	8:22 PM	(3.06) **H**
8:41 AM	(3.62) **H**	3:10 PM	(1.16) L	8:46 PM	(3.07) **H**
9:04 AM	(3.49) **H**	3:19 PM	(1.21) L	9:11 PM	(3.04) **H**
9:26 AM	(3.32) **H**	3:26 PM	(1.24) L	9:35 PM	(2.98) **H**
9:44 AM	(3.11) **H**	3:35 PM	(1.28) L	10:01 PM	(2.88) **H**
9:58 AM	(2.87) **H**	3:48 PM	(1.34) L	10:30 PM	(2.76) **H**
10:05 AM	(2.63) **H**	4:03 PM	(1.42) L	11:07 PM	(2.62) **H**
10:01 AM	(2.40) **H**	4:18 PM	(1.54) L		
3:47 AM	(2.25) L	6:05 AM	(2.33) **H**	4:30 PM	(1.69) L
4:02 PM	(1.85) L	6:23 PM	(1.88) **H**	8:35 PM	(1.84) L
12:30 PM	(1.71) L	5:38 PM	(2.06) **H**	10:52 PM	(1.66) L
12:40 PM	(1.53) L	5:48 PM	(2.28) **H**	11:38 PM	(1.41) L
12:59 PM	(1.36) L	6:09 PM	(2.54) **H**		
6:44 AM	(3.45) **H**	1:22 PM	(1.18) L	6:35 PM	(2.82) **H**
7:08 AM	(3.68) **H**	1:46 PM	(1.00) L	7:05 PM	(3.12) **H**
7:34 AM	(3.87) **H**	2:12 PM	(0.83) L	7:40 PM	(3.38) **H**
8:04 AM	(3.96) **H**	2:38 PM	(0.69) L	8:19 PM	(3.58) **H**
8:36 AM	(3.93) **H**	3:06 PM	(0.61) L	9:02 PM	(3.68) **H**
9:12 AM	(3.74) **H**	3:36 PM	(0.64) L	9:48 PM	(3.65) **H**
9:48 AM	(3.40) **H**	4:11 PM	(0.77) L	10:39 PM	(3.51) **H**

TIDE TIMES

Tim Smith's

POPULAR TIDE ADJUSTMENTS

Abbot Point	+40min
Cairns	+ 5min
Lucinda	0
Mackay Outer Harbour	+2hr 25min
Mourilyan Low tide	-15min
Mourilyan High tide	+5min
Port Douglas Low Tide	-20min
Port Douglas High Tide	0
Shute Harbour	+ 2hr 5min
Bowen	+ 35min
Cooktown	0
Flinders Reef	- 20min

Townsville

Day	Date	Tide 1	
Tue	1	4:53 AM	(1.42) L
Wed	2	6:30 AM	(1.77) L
THu	3	12:57 AM	(3.03) H
Fri	4	3:29 AM	(3.02) H
Sat	5	5:02 AM	(3.23) H
Sun	6	5:51 AM	(3.40) H
Mon	7	12:14 AM	(1.13) L
Tue	8	12:55 AM	(1.04) L
Wed	9	1:27 AM	(1.03) L
THu	10	1:52 AM	(1.07) L
Fri	11	2:13 AM	(1.16) L
Sat	12	2:30 AM	(1.27) L
Sun	13 ○	2:49 AM	(1.40) L
Mon	14	3:09 AM	(1.55) L
Tue	15	3:28 AM	(1.72) L
Wed	16	3:46 AM	(1.90) L
THu	17	6:04 AM	(2.08) L
Fri	18	4:24 PM	(1.54) L
Sat	19	1:19 AM	(2.58) H
Sun	20	4:30 AM	(2.72) H
Mon	21	5:04 AM	(2.95) H
Tue	22	5:31 AM	(3.18) H
Wed	23	5:59 AM	(3.39) H
THu	24	12:15 AM	(1.04) L
Fri	25	12:54 AM	(0.89) L
Sat	26	1:33 AM	(0.83) L
Sun	27	2:16 AM	(0.87) L
Mon	28 ●	3:07 AM	(1.02) L
Tue	29	4:09 AM	(1.25) L
Wed	30	5:21 AM	(1.48) L

Tide 2		Tide 3		Tide 4	
10:28 AM	(2.97) H	4:53 PM	(0.99) L	11:37 PM	(3.27) H
11:15 AM	(2.50) H	6:01 PM	(1.27) L		
8:53 AM	(1.86) L	12:40 PM	(2.08) H	7:56 PM	(1.49) L
11:00 AM	(1.59) L	4:23 PM	(2.09) H	10:02 PM	(1.46) L
11:57 AM	(1.30) L	5:38 PM	(2.36) H	11:19 PM	(1.28) L
12:36 PM	(1.12) L	6:17 PM	(2.60) H		
6:26 AM	(3.48) H	1:11 PM	(1.03) L	6:48 PM	(2.78) H
6:55 AM	(3.50) H	1:40 PM	(1.01) L	7:15 PM	(2.91) H
7:19 AM	(3.48) H	2:02 PM	(1.03) L	7:40 PM	(3.01) H
7:43 AM	(3.41) H	2:19 PM	(1.06) L	8:05 PM	(3.07) H
8:03 AM	(3.32) H	2:29 PM	(1.07) L	8:30 PM	(3.11) H
8:22 AM	(3.18) H	2:33 PM	(1.06) L	8:55 PM	(3.11) H
8:39 AM	(3.02) H	2:42 PM	(1.05) L	9:20 PM	(3.09) H
8:54 AM	(2.85) H	2:56 PM	(1.07) L	9:47 PM	(3.04) H
9:08 AM	(2.66) H	3:14 PM	(1.12) L	10:19 PM	(2.95) H
9:23 AM	(2.46) H	3:33 PM	(1.22) L	10:57 PM	(2.83) H
9:33 AM	(2.25) H	3:56 PM	(1.37) L	11:50 PM	(2.69) H
11:50 AM	(1.82) L	1:11 PM	(1.83) H	7:05 PM	(1.73) L
11:35 AM	(1.63) L	4:23 PM	(2.00) H	9:30 PM	(1.67) L
11:54 AM	(1.44) L	5:04 PM	(2.26) H	10:47 PM	(1.47) L
12:18 PM	(1.24) L	5:37 PM	(2.55) H	11:35 PM	(1.24) L
12:45 PM	(1.03) L	6:11 PM	(2.86) H		
6:26 AM	(3.57) H	1:11 PM	(0.82) L	6:46 PM	(3.18) H
6:55 AM	(3.68) H	1:37 PM	(0.63) L	7:25 PM	(3.47) H
7:28 AM	(3.70) H	2:05 PM	(0.48) L	8:08 PM	(3.69) H
8:03 AM	(3.58) H	2:36 PM	(0.42) L	8:53 PM	(3.80) H
8:42 AM	(3.34) H	3:10 PM	(0.47) L	9:42 PM	(3.80) H
9:24 AM	(3.00) H	3:50 PM	(0.63) L	10:34 PM	(3.67) H
10:13 AM	(2.62) H	4:41 PM	(0.87) L	11:32 PM	(3.45) H

TIDE TIMES

Tim Smith's

Townsville

POPULAR TIDE ADJUSTMENTS

Abbot Point	+40min
Cairns	+ 5min
Lucinda	0
Mackay Outer Harbour	+2hr 25min
Mourilyan Low tide	-15min
Mourilyan High tide	+5min
Port Douglas Low Tide	-20min
Port Douglas High Tide	0
Shute Harbour	+ 2hr 5min
Bowen	+ 35min
Cooktown	0
Flinders Reef	- 20min

Day	Date	Tide 1	
THu	1	6:51 AM	(1.64) L
Fri	2	12:47 AM	(3.23) H
Sat	3	2:37 AM	(3.11) H
Sun	4	4:10 AM	(3.15) H
Mon	5	5:07 AM	(3.21) H
Tue	6	5:46 AM	(3.22) H
Wed	7	12:30 AM	(1.30) L
THu	8	1:07 AM	(1.32) L
Fri	9	1:39 AM	(1.37) L
Sat	10	2:06 AM	(1.44) L
Sun	11	2:31 AM	(1.51) L
Mon	12	2:59 AM	(1.58) L
Tue	13 ○	3:30 AM	(1.66) L
Wed	14	4:10 AM	(1.75) L
THu	15	5:04 AM	(1.83) L
Fri	16	6:13 AM	(1.90) L
Sat	17	7:56 AM	(1.88) L
Sun	18	12:49 AM	(2.81) H
Mon	19	2:20 AM	(2.82) H
Tue	20	3:42 AM	(2.93) H
Wed	21	4:31 AM	(3.08) H
THu	22	5:10 AM	(3.20) H
Fri	23	5:45 AM	(3.28) H
Sat	24	12:45 AM	(1.18) L
Sun	25	1:36 AM	(1.12) L
Mon	26	2:30 AM	(1.12) L
Tue	27 ●	3:25 AM	(1.16) L
Wed	28	4:24 AM	(1.25) L
THu	29	5:29 AM	(1.35) L
Fri	30	6:42 AM	(1.42) L
Sat	31	12:23 AM	(3.35) H

Tide 2		Tide 3		Tide 4	
11:16 AM	(2.24) H	5:49 PM	(1.15) L		
8:42 AM	(1.61) L	1:10 PM	(1.99) H	7:27 PM	(1.38) L
10:15 AM	(1.43) L	3:36 PM	(2.08) H	9:19 PM	(1.45) L
11:16 AM	(1.24) L	4:55 PM	(2.30) H	10:41 PM	(1.39) L
12:00 PM	(1.11) L	5:45 PM	(2.52) H	11:42 PM	(1.33) L
12:37 PM	(1.04) L	6:24 PM	(2.69) H		
6:17 AM	(3.19) H	1:07 PM	(1.02) L	6:56 PM	(2.82) H
6:44 AM	(3.12) H	1:30 PM	(1.02) L	7:26 PM	(2.93) H
7:06 AM	(3.04) H	1:44 PM	(1.02) L	7:53 PM	(3.02) H
7:25 AM	(2.93) H	1:51 PM	(1.00) L	8:19 PM	(3.08) H
7:43 AM	(2.82) H	1:59 PM	(0.96) L	8:45 PM	(3.12) H
8:00 AM	(2.70) H	2:13 PM	(0.94) L	9:12 PM	(3.14) H
8:20 AM	(2.57) H	2:33 PM	(0.94) L	9:42 PM	(3.12) H
8:45 AM	(2.44) H	2:59 PM	(0.99) L	10:15 PM	(3.07) H
9:15 AM	(2.29) H	3:29 PM	(1.09) L	10:56 PM	(2.99) H
9:53 AM	(2.14) H	4:06 PM	(1.22) L	11:45 PM	(2.89) H
11:01 AM	(1.98) H	5:02 PM	(1.37) L		
9:32 AM	(1.74) L	1:02 PM	(1.91) H	6:35 PM	(1.50) L
10:22 AM	(1.55) L	3:02 PM	(2.02) H	8:19 PM	(1.55) L
11:00 AM	(1.35) L	4:14 PM	(2.25) H	9:49 PM	(1.49) L
11:33 AM	(1.13) L	5:04 PM	(2.54) H	10:58 PM	(1.38) L
12:05 PM	(0.92) L	5:49 PM	(2.85) H	11:53 PM	(1.27) L
12:37 PM	(0.71) L	6:32 PM	(3.17) H		
6:20 AM	(3.30) H	1:08 PM	(0.54) L	7:17 PM	(3.46) H
6:59 AM	(3.24) H	1:42 PM	(0.41) L	8:03 PM	(3.69) H
7:41 AM	(3.11) H	2:18 PM	(0.37) L	8:50 PM	(3.82) H
8:27 AM	(2.91) H	3:00 PM	(0.41) L	9:40 PM	(3.85) H
9:17 AM	(2.67) H	3:47 PM	(0.54) L	10:30 PM	(3.76) H
10:15 AM	(2.43) H	4:40 PM	(0.75) L	11:24 PM	(3.58) H
11:23 AM	(2.21) H	5:38 PM	(0.99) L		
8:00 AM	(1.44) L	12:49 PM	(2.08) H	6:48 PM	(1.23) L

TIDE TIMES

POPULAR TIDE ADJUSTMENTS

Abbot Point	+40min
Cairns	+ 5min
Lucinda	0
Mackay Outer Harbour	+2hr 25min
Mourilyan Low tide	-15min
Mourilyan High tide	+5min
Port Douglas Low Tide	-20min
Port Douglas High Tide	0
Shute Harbour	+ 2hr 5min
Bowen	+ 35min
Cooktown	0
Flinders Reef	- 20min

Townsville

Day	Date	Tide 1	
Sun	1	1:34 AM	(3.14) H
Mon	2	2:55 AM	(3.00) H
Tue	3	4:04 AM	(2.92) H
Wed	4	4:57 AM	(2.86) H
THu	5	12:07 AM	(1.58) L
Fri	6	12:55 AM	(1.57) L
Sat	7	1:35 AM	(1.57) L
Sun	8	2:08 AM	(1.57) L
Mon	9	2:38 AM	(1.57) L
Tue	10	3:08 AM	(1.57) L
Wed	11 ○	3:40 AM	(1.58) L
THu	12	4:16 AM	(1.60) L
Fri	13	5:00 AM	(1.63) L
Sat	14	5:53 AM	(1.65) L
Sun	15	6:55 AM	(1.64) L
Mon	16	12:21 AM	(3.04) H
Tue	17	1:16 AM	(2.97) H
Wed	18	2:22 AM	(2.92) H
THu	19	3:29 AM	(2.89) H
Fri	20	4:26 AM	(2.87) H
Sat	21	5:15 AM	(2.85) H
Sun	22	1:00 AM	(1.37) L
Mon	23	1:54 AM	(1.25) L
Tue	24	2:45 AM	(1.15) L
Wed	25 ●	3:33 AM	(1.11) L
THu	26	4:22 AM	(1.12) L
Fri	27	5:14 AM	(1.18) L
Sat	28	6:09 AM	(1.27) L
Sun	29	7:09 AM	(1.36) L
Mon	30	12:35 AM	(3.12) H

Tide 2		Tide 3		Tide 4	
9:17 AM	(1.38) L	2:33 PM	(2.08) H	8:20 PM	(1.43) L
10:24 AM	(1.29) L	3:59 PM	(2.19) H	9:47 PM	(1.54) L
11:18 AM	(1.20) L	5:09 PM	(2.36) H	11:04 PM	(1.58) L
12:00 PM	(1.12) L	6:02 PM	(2.54) H		
5:35 AM	(2.79) H	12:31 PM	(1.07) L	6:44 PM	(2.70) H
6:06 AM	(2.72) H	12:55 PM	(1.04) L	7:17 PM	(2.85) H
6:32 AM	(2.64) H	1:11 PM	(1.01) L	7:46 PM	(2.96) H
6:54 AM	(2.56) H	1:23 PM	(0.97) L	8:13 PM	(3.06) H
7:15 AM	(2.49) H	1:37 PM	(0.92) L	8:38 PM	(3.13) H
7:39 AM	(2.44) H	1:58 PM	(0.87) L	9:05 PM	(3.18) H
8:07 AM	(2.40) H	2:26 PM	(0.84) L	9:36 PM	(3.21) H
8:41 AM	(2.35) H	2:59 PM	(0.85) L	10:10 PM	(3.21) H
9:22 AM	(2.28) H	3:36 PM	(0.90) L	10:49 PM	(3.17) H
10:14 AM	(2.21) H	4:18 PM	(0.99) L	11:32 PM	(3.12) H
11:20 AM	(2.13) H	5:08 PM	(1.12) L		
8:04 AM	(1.58) L	12:35 PM	(2.09) H	6:08 PM	(1.28) L
9:08 AM	(1.44) L	2:00 PM	(2.12) H	7:27 PM	(1.44) L
10:02 AM	(1.26) L	3:29 PM	(2.28) H	9:01 PM	(1.55) L
10:49 AM	(1.07) L	4:41 PM	(2.53) H	10:34 PM	(1.57) L
11:32 AM	(0.88) L	5:40 PM	(2.84) H	11:55 PM	(1.50) L
12:12 PM	(0.70) L	6:31 PM	(3.15) H		
6:02 AM	(2.82) H	12:51 PM	(0.55) L	7:19 PM	(3.44) H
6:49 AM	(2.78) H	1:31 PM	(0.44) L	8:05 PM	(3.67) H
7:38 AM	(2.72) H	2:14 PM	(0.38) L	8:50 PM	(3.82) H
8:29 AM	(2.65) H	2:58 PM	(0.38) L	9:35 PM	(3.86) H
9:20 AM	(2.57) H	3:43 PM	(0.47) L	10:19 PM	(3.79) H
10:13 AM	(2.46) H	4:28 PM	(0.63) L	11:04 PM	(3.63) H
11:06 AM	(2.34) H	5:12 PM	(0.86) L	11:49 PM	(3.39) H
12:04 PM	(2.21) H	5:58 PM	(1.14) L		
8:15 AM	(1.41) L	1:17 PM	(2.11) H	6:54 PM	(1.45) L

TIDE TIMES

Tim Smith's

Townsville

POPULAR TIDE ADJUSTMENTS

Abbot Point	+40min
Cairns	+ 5min
Lucinda	0
Mackay Outer Harbour	+2hr 25min
Mourilyan Low tide	-15min
Mourilyan High tide	+5min
Port Douglas Low Tide	-20min
Port Douglas High Tide	0
Shute Harbour	+ 2hr 5min
Bowen	+ 35min
Cooktown	0
Flinders Reef	- 20min

Day	Date	Tide 1	
Tue	1	1:28 AM	(2.86) **H**
Wed	2	2:32 AM	(2.63) **H**
THu	3	3:45 AM	(2.48) **H**
Fri	4	4:50 AM	(2.39) **H**
Sat	5	12:56 AM	(1.69) L
Sun	6	1:37 AM	(1.60) L
Mon	7	2:09 AM	(1.53) L
Tue	8	2:36 AM	(1.47) L
Wed	9	3:02 AM	(1.43) L
THu	10	3:30 AM	(1.39) L
Fri	11 ○	4:00 AM	(1.37) L
Sat	12	4:36 AM	(1.37) L
Sun	13	5:17 AM	(1.37) L
Mon	14	6:05 AM	(1.38) L
Tue	15	7:01 AM	(1.36) L
Wed	16	12:30 AM	(3.04) **H**
THu	17	1:23 AM	(2.82) **H**
Fri	18	2:33 AM	(2.60) **H**
Sat	19	4:03 AM	(2.46) **H**
Sun	20	12:23 AM	(1.54) L
Mon	21	1:20 AM	(1.33) L
Tue	22	2:07 AM	(1.14) L
Wed	23	2:47 AM	(1.02) L
THu	24	3:27 AM	(0.97) L
Fri	25 ●	4:04 AM	(0.99) L
Sat	26	4:42 AM	(1.08) L
Sun	27	5:20 AM	(1.20) L
Mon	28	6:01 AM	(1.33) L
Tue	29	6:50 AM	(1.44) L
Wed	30	12:15 AM	(2.71) **H**
THu	31	12:55 AM	(2.41) **H**

Tide 2		Tide 3		Tide 4	
9:23 AM	(1.40) L	2:56 PM	(2.09) H	8:33 PM	(1.71) L
10:27 AM	(1.34) L	4:38 PM	(2.22) H	10:28 PM	(1.83) L
11:17 AM	(1.25) L	5:58 PM	(2.43) H	11:59 PM	(1.79) L
11:55 AM	(1.17) L	6:42 PM	(2.64) H		
5:38 AM	(2.34) H	12:22 PM	(1.11) L	7:13 PM	(2.81) H
6:13 AM	(2.31) H	12:44 PM	(1.04) L	7:38 PM	(2.95) H
6:40 AM	(2.30) H	1:03 PM	(0.97) L	8:02 PM	(3.07) H
7:05 AM	(2.32) H	1:24 PM	(0.87) L	8:27 PM	(3.17) H
7:32 AM	(2.36) H	1:50 PM	(0.78) L	8:53 PM	(3.27) H
8:03 AM	(2.42) H	2:21 PM	(0.70) L	9:23 PM	(3.35) H
8:40 AM	(2.46) H	2:55 PM	(0.65) L	9:55 PM	(3.40) H
9:22 AM	(2.47) H	3:30 PM	(0.67) L	10:30 PM	(3.40) H
10:10 AM	(2.44) H	4:08 PM	(0.76) L	11:07 PM	(3.34) H
11:05 AM	(2.38) H	4:49 PM	(0.93) L	11:46 PM	(3.22) H
12:06 PM	(2.32) H	5:39 PM	(1.17) L		
8:04 AM	(1.31) L	1:18 PM	(2.28) H	6:51 PM	(1.46) L
9:09 AM	(1.21) L	2:58 PM	(2.35) H	8:43 PM	(1.70) L
10:14 AM	(1.07) L	4:36 PM	(2.59) H	10:54 PM	(1.72) L
11:12 AM	(0.91) L	5:47 PM	(2.90) H		
5:18 AM	(2.43) H	12:03 PM	(0.75) L	6:41 PM	(3.22) H
6:16 AM	(2.46) H	12:49 PM	(0.60) L	7:25 PM	(3.49) H
7:04 AM	(2.53) H	1:32 PM	(0.47) L	8:04 PM	(3.69) H
7:48 AM	(2.60) H	2:13 PM	(0.38) L	8:43 PM	(3.81) H
8:30 AM	(2.66) H	2:51 PM	(0.37) L	9:20 PM	(3.83) H
9:12 AM	(2.66) H	3:27 PM	(0.44) L	9:58 PM	(3.75) H
9:52 AM	(2.61) H	4:00 PM	(0.61) L	10:33 PM	(3.57) H
10:33 AM	(2.49) H	4:30 PM	(0.86) L	11:08 PM	(3.32) H
11:16 AM	(2.35) H	5:00 PM	(1.17) L	11:41 PM	(3.02) H
12:07 PM	(2.19) H	5:27 PM	(1.51) L		
7:55 AM	(1.51) L	1:25 PM	(2.07) H	6:14 PM	(1.84) L
9:15 AM	(1.51) L	5:50 PM	(2.15) H	10:18 PM	(2.00) L

TIDE TIMES

Tim Smith's

Townsville

POPULAR TIDE ADJUSTMENTS

Abbot Point	+40min
Cairns	+ 5min
Lucinda	0
Mackay Outer Harbour	+2hr 25min
Mourilyan Low tide	-15min
Mourilyan High tide	+5min
Port Douglas Low Tide	-20min
Port Douglas High Tide	0
Shute Harbour	+ 2hr 5min
Bowen	+ 35min
Cooktown	0
Flinders Reef	- 20min

Day	Date		Tide 1	
Fri	1		2:02 AM	(2.16) **H**
Sat	2		12:18 AM	(1.83) L
Sun	3		1:02 AM	(1.65) L
Mon	4		1:31 AM	(1.50) L
Tue	5		1:56 AM	(1.40) L
Wed	6		2:17 AM	(1.31) L
THu	7		2:40 AM	(1.24) L
Fri	8		3:04 AM	(1.17) L
Sat	9	○	3:30 AM	(1.11) L
Sun	10		4:00 AM	(1.07) L
Mon	11		4:33 AM	(1.06) L
Tue	12		5:13 AM	(1.08) L
Wed	13		6:02 AM	(1.13) L
THu	14		7:05 AM	(1.19) L
Fri	15		12:36 AM	(2.57) **H**
Sat	16		2:00 AM	(2.22) **H**
Sun	17		4:40 AM	(2.14) **H**
Mon	18		12:43 AM	(1.33) L
Tue	19		1:26 AM	(1.09) L
Wed	20		2:02 AM	(0.94) L
THu	21		2:35 AM	(0.87) L
Fri	22		3:05 AM	(0.87) L
Sat	23	●	3:32 AM	(0.92) L
Sun	24		3:58 AM	(1.01) L
Mon	25		4:18 AM	(1.11) L
Tue	26		4:34 AM	(1.23) L
Wed	27		4:46 AM	(1.33) L
THu	28		4:57 AM	(1.44) L
Fri	29		5:11 AM	(1.55) L
Sat	30		8:38 AM	(1.61) L
Sun	31		12:47 AM	(1.72) L

Tide 2		Tide 3		Tide 4	
10:28 AM	(1.43) L	6:19 PM	(2.41) H		
4:15 AM	(2.04) H	11:18 AM	(1.33) L	6:40 PM	(2.63) H
5:38 AM	(2.06) H	11:54 AM	(1.21) L	7:00 PM	(2.82) H
6:14 AM	(2.13) H	12:22 PM	(1.10) L	7:21 PM	(2.97) H
6:39 AM	(2.21) H	12:47 PM	(0.96) L	7:42 PM	(3.12) H
7:00 AM	(2.32) H	1:12 PM	(0.81) L	8:04 PM	(3.26) H
7:25 AM	(2.46) H	1:39 PM	(0.66) L	8:30 PM	(3.40) H
7:54 AM	(2.60) H	2:08 PM	(0.54) L	8:57 PM	(3.52) H
8:29 AM	(2.71) H	2:39 PM	(0.47) L	9:27 PM	(3.59) H
9:09 AM	(2.77) H	3:12 PM	(0.50) L	9:58 PM	(3.58) H
9:54 AM	(2.76) H	3:47 PM	(0.64) L	10:31 PM	(3.47) H
10:45 AM	(2.70) H	4:27 PM	(0.90) L	11:08 PM	(3.25) H
11:41 AM	(2.59) H	5:16 PM	(1.25) L	11:47 PM	(2.93) H
12:51 PM	(2.48) H	6:51 PM	(1.63) L		
8:24 AM	(1.21) L	2:49 PM	(2.48) H	9:18 PM	(1.82) L
9:51 AM	(1.13) L	4:49 PM	(2.74) H	11:40 PM	(1.62) L
11:06 AM	(0.97) L	5:58 PM	(3.08) H		
5:56 AM	(2.27) H	12:04 PM	(0.78) L	6:43 PM	(3.36) H
6:41 AM	(2.43) H	12:50 PM	(0.61) L	7:19 PM	(3.57) H
7:15 AM	(2.58) H	1:30 PM	(0.48) L	7:52 PM	(3.69) H
7:47 AM	(2.70) H	2:04 PM	(0.42) L	8:24 PM	(3.74) H
8:20 AM	(2.78) H	2:34 PM	(0.45) L	8:55 PM	(3.71) H
8:52 AM	(2.80) H	3:01 PM	(0.56) L	9:26 PM	(3.59) H
9:25 AM	(2.75) H	3:26 PM	(0.75) L	9:54 PM	(3.39) H
9:58 AM	(2.64) H	3:46 PM	(1.01) L	10:21 PM	(3.14) H
10:31 AM	(2.50) H	4:03 PM	(1.31) L	10:45 PM	(2.84) H
11:13 AM	(2.34) H	4:15 PM	(1.61) L	11:04 PM	(2.54) H
12:07 PM	(2.20) H	4:15 PM	(1.91) L	11:13 PM	(2.24) H
6:03 PM	(2.21) H				
6:08 PM	(2.44) H				
5:29 AM	(1.81) H	10:38 AM	(1.49) L	6:18 PM	(2.65)

TIDE TIMES

Tim Smith's

Townsville

POPULAR TIDE ADJUSTMENTS

Abbot Point	+40min
Cairns	+ 5min
Lucinda	0
Mackay Outer Harbour	+2hr 25min
Mourilyan Low tide	-15min
Mourilyan High tide	+5min
Port Douglas Low Tide	-20min
Port Douglas High Tide	0
Shute Harbour	+ 2hr 5min
Bowen	+ 35min
Cooktown	0
Flinders Reef	- 20min

Day	Date	Tide 1		
Mon	1		12:53 AM	(1.53) L
Tue	2		1:08 AM	(1.38) L
Wed	3		1:26 AM	(1.26) L
THu	4		1:45 AM	(1.15) L
Fri	5		2:07 AM	(1.04) L
Sat	6		2:30 AM	(0.93) L
Sun	7		2:53 AM	(0.83) L
Mon	8	○	3:18 AM	(0.75) L
Tue	9		3:46 AM	(0.73) L
Wed	10		4:18 AM	(0.78) L
THu	11		5:00 AM	(0.91) L
Fri	12		6:08 AM	(1.10) L
Sat	13		12:02 AM	(2.22) H
Sun	14		3:09 AM	(1.91) H
Mon	15		5:16 AM	(2.11) H
Tue	16		12:34 AM	(1.05) L
Wed	17		1:11 AM	(0.87) L
THu	18		1:43 AM	(0.79) L
Fri	19		2:12 AM	(0.78) L
Sat	20		2:35 AM	(0.81) L
Sun	21		2:54 AM	(0.87) L
Mon	22	●	3:06 AM	(0.92) L
Tue	23		3:14 AM	(0.98) L
Wed	24		3:20 AM	(1.04) L
THu	25		3:31 AM	(1.11) L
Fri	26		3:45 AM	(1.22) L
Sat	27		3:59 AM	(1.36) L
Sun	28		3:58 AM	(1.52) L
Mon	29		12:43 AM	(1.60) L
Tue	30		12:20 AM	(1.44) L

Tide 2		Tide 3		Tide 4	
5:52 AM	(1.95) H	11:25 AM	(1.33) L	6:33 PM	(2.83) H
6:10 AM	(2.09) H	11:58 AM	(1.16) L	6:51 PM	(3.00) H
6:27 AM	(2.26) H	12:26 PM	(0.97) L	7:10 PM	(3.17) H
6:45 AM	(2.44) H	12:52 PM	(0.78) L	7:31 PM	(3.35) H
7:09 AM	(2.65) H	1:18 PM	(0.60) L	7:55 PM	(3.51) H
7:37 AM	(2.84) H	1:46 PM	(0.47) L	8:21 PM	(3.64) H
8:12 AM	(3.00) H	2:16 PM	(0.43) L	8:49 PM	(3.68) H
8:51 AM	(3.10) H	2:50 PM	(0.51) L	9:20 PM	(3.61) H
9:36 AM	(3.10) H	3:28 PM	(0.72) L	9:53 PM	(3.41) H
10:26 AM	(3.02) H	4:12 PM	(1.06) L	10:29 PM	(3.09) H
11:23 AM	(2.87) H	5:27 PM	(1.46) L	11:09 PM	(2.67) H
12:36 PM	(2.70) H	7:30 PM	(1.76) L		
7:47 AM	(1.23) L	2:57 PM	(2.68) H	10:23 PM	(1.68) L
9:40 AM	(1.19) L	4:50 PM	(2.96) H	11:49 PM	(1.34) L
11:00 AM	(1.00) L	5:47 PM	(3.25) H		
6:04 AM	(2.35) H	11:58 AM	(0.80) L	6:28 PM	(3.45) H
6:39 AM	(2.56) H	12:42 PM	(0.65) L	7:00 PM	(3.56) H
7:08 AM	(2.72) H	1:18 PM	(0.58) L	7:29 PM	(3.59) H
7:35 AM	(2.83) H	1:48 PM	(0.60) L	7:56 PM	(3.57) H
8:02 AM	(2.90) H	2:14 PM	(0.68) L	8:22 PM	(3.48) H
8:31 AM	(2.91) H	2:35 PM	(0.83) L	8:47 PM	(3.33) H
9:00 AM	(2.87) H	2:56 PM	(1.03) L	9:10 PM	(3.12) H
9:29 AM	(2.79) H	3:13 PM	(1.26) L	9:28 PM	(2.88) H
10:00 AM	(2.68) H	3:28 PM	(1.50) L	9:42 PM	(2.62) H
10:35 AM	(2.55) H	3:39 PM	(1.75) L	9:48 PM	(2.36) H
11:21 AM	(2.40) H	3:45 PM	(1.98) L	9:33 PM	(2.13) H
12:32 PM	(2.27) H	3:24 PM	(2.19) L	5:22 PM	(2.24) H
5:30 PM	(2.44) H				
5:56 AM	(1.73) H	9:12 AM	(1.63) L	5:40 PM	(2.63) H
5:38 AM	(1.91) H	10:44 AM	(1.45) L	5:53 PM	(2.82) H

TIDE TIMES

Tim Smith's

Townsville

Day	Date	Tide 1		
Wed	1	12:31 AM	(1.29)	L
THu	2	12:48 AM	(1.15)	L
Fri	3	1:08 AM	(1.00)	L
Sat	4	1:30 AM	(0.85)	L
Sun	5	1:52 AM	(0.70)	L
Mon	6	2:15 AM	(0.56)	L
Tue	7	2:39 AM	(0.46)	L
Wed	8	3:06 AM	(0.45)	L
THu	9	3:38 AM	(0.54)	L
Fri	10	4:18 AM	(0.74)	L
Sat	11	5:29 AM	(1.02)	L
Sun	12	12:03 AM	(1.95)	**H**
Mon	13	3:37 AM	(1.89)	**H**
Tue	14	5:02 AM	(2.18)	**H**
Wed	15	12:08 AM	(0.92)	L
THu	16	12:44 AM	(0.79)	L
Fri	17	1:15 AM	(0.74)	L
Sat	18	1:43 AM	(0.75)	L
Sun	19	2:02 AM	(0.79)	L
Mon	20	2:15 AM	(0.82)	L
Tue	21	2:21 AM	(0.84)	L
Wed	22	2:28 AM	(0.86)	L
THu	23	2:40 AM	(0.89)	L
Fri	24	2:58 AM	(0.97)	L
Sat	25	3:16 AM	(1.08)	L
Sun	26	3:37 AM	(1.24)	L
Mon	27	3:56 AM	(1.43)	L
Tue	28	5:10 AM	(1.64)	**H**
Wed	29	4:40 AM	(1.86)	**H**
THu	30	5:03 AM	(2.10)	**H**
Fri	31	12:06 AM	(1.10)	L

OCTOBER 2025

Tide 2		Tide 3		Tide 4	
5:45 AM	(2.11) **H**	11:24 AM	(1.24) **L**	6:10 PM	(3.01) **H**
6:01 AM	(2.33) **H**	11:55 AM	(1.04) **L**	6:30 PM	(3.20) **H**
6:22 AM	(2.57) **H**	12:24 PM	(0.84) **L**	6:50 PM	(3.38) **H**
6:48 AM	(2.82) **H**	12:53 PM	(0.68) **L**	7:14 PM	(3.53) **H**
7:19 AM	(3.07) **H**	1:24 PM	(0.59) **L**	7:39 PM	(3.62) **H**
7:55 AM	(3.27) **H**	1:58 PM	(0.59) **L**	8:09 PM	(3.61) **H**
8:36 AM	(3.40) **H**	2:36 PM	(0.71) **L**	8:42 PM	(3.46) **H**
9:23 AM	(3.41) **H**	3:23 PM	(0.95) **L**	9:17 PM	(3.18) **H**
10:15 AM	(3.32) **H**	4:31 PM	(1.27) **L**	9:58 PM	(2.80) **H**
11:14 AM	(3.15) **H**	6:06 PM	(1.56) **L**	10:45 PM	(2.36) **H**
12:30 PM	(2.96) **H**	8:07 PM	(1.66) **L**		
7:22 AM	(1.23) **L**	2:41 PM	(2.92) **H**	10:17 PM	(1.43) **L**
9:21 AM	(1.21) **L**	4:20 PM	(3.11) **H**	11:24 PM	(1.13) **L**
10:41 AM	(1.06) **L**	5:18 PM	(3.29) **H**		
5:47 AM	(2.44) **H**	11:38 AM	(0.91) **L**	5:59 PM	(3.39) **H**
6:22 AM	(2.65) **H**	12:24 PM	(0.84) **L**	6:30 PM	(3.41) **H**
6:52 AM	(2.80) **H**	1:01 PM	(0.84) **L**	6:58 PM	(3.37) **H**
7:20 AM	(2.90) **H**	1:33 PM	(0.91) **L**	7:23 PM	(3.29) **H**
7:48 AM	(2.96) **H**	2:00 PM	(1.03) **L**	7:45 PM	(3.16) **H**
8:16 AM	(2.98) **H**	2:23 PM	(1.18) **L**	8:06 PM	(3.01) **H**
8:44 AM	(2.97) **H**	2:45 PM	(1.33) **L**	8:24 PM	(2.82) **H**
9:12 AM	(2.93) **H**	3:10 PM	(1.50) **L**	8:39 PM	(2.63) **H**
9:42 AM	(2.86) **H**	3:41 PM	(1.68) **L**	8:53 PM	(2.43) **H**
10:16 AM	(2.76) **H**	4:49 PM	(1.85) **L**	9:07 PM	(2.23) **H**
11:00 AM	(2.64) **H**	6:25 PM	(1.96) **I**	9:11 PM	(2.03) **H**
11:58 AM	(2.51) **H**				
1:46 PM	(2.45) **H**	11:47 PM	(1.61) **L**		
7:17 AM	(1.61) **L**	4:23 PM	(2.61) **H**	11:30 PM	(1.45) **L**
9:27 AM	(1.54) **L**	4:51 PM	(2.80) **H**	11:45 PM	(1.27) **L**
10:32 AM	(1.38) **L**	5:15 PM	(2.99) **H**		
5:30 AM	(2.36) **H**	11:16 AM	(1.20) **L**	5:40 PM	(3.16) **H**

TIDE TIMES

Tim Smith's

Townsville

POPULAR TIDE ADJUSTMENTS

Abbot Point	+40min
Cairns	+ 5min
Lucinda	0
Mackay Outer Harbour	+2hr 25min
Mourilyan Low tide	-15min
Mourilyan High tide	+5min
Port Douglas Low Tide	-20min
Port Douglas High Tide	0
Shute Harbour	+ 2hr 5min
Bowen	+ 35min
Cooktown	0
Flinders Reef	- 20min

Day	Date	Tide 1	
Sat	1	12:30 AM	(0.91) L
Sun	2	12:53 AM	(0.72) L
Mon	3	1:17 AM	(0.54) L
Tue	4	1:43 AM	(0.38) L
Wed	5 ○	2:10 AM	(0.29) L
THu	6	2:42 AM	(0.30) L
Fri	7	3:20 AM	(0.42) L
Sat	8	4:09 AM	(0.64) L
Sun	9	5:19 AM	(0.91) L
Mon	10	12:20 AM	(1.94) H
Tue	11	2:54 AM	(1.96) H
Wed	12	4:21 AM	(2.19) H
THu	13	5:19 AM	(2.43) H
Fri	14	12:14 AM	(0.86) L
Sat	15	12:47 AM	(0.81) L
Sun	16	1:14 AM	(0.80) L
Mon	17	1:32 AM	(0.81) L
Tue	18	1:43 AM	(0.82) L
Wed	19	1:50 AM	(0.82) L
THu	20 ●	2:02 AM	(0.81) L
Fri	21	2:22 AM	(0.83) L
Sat	22	2:46 AM	(0.89) L
Sun	23	3:14 AM	(0.99) L
Mon	24	3:46 AM	(1.13) L
Tue	25	4:30 AM	(1.30) L
Wed	26	12:22 AM	(1.79) H
THu	27	2:49 AM	(1.86) H
Fri	28	4:07 AM	(2.09) H
Sat	29	4:55 AM	(2.37) H
Sun	30	5:37 AM	(2.69) H

NOVEMBER 2025

Tide 2		Tide 3		Tide 4	
5:58 AM	(2.65) H	11:54 AM	(1.04) L	6:04 PM	(3.30) H
6:30 AM	(2.94) H	12:31 PM	(0.93) L	6:30 PM	(3.40) H
7:04 AM	(3.23) H	1:10 PM	(0.87) L	7:00 PM	(3.43) H
7:44 AM	(3.47) H	1:53 PM	(0.88) L	7:34 PM	(3.36) H
8:28 AM	(3.62) H	2:43 PM	(0.98) L	8:13 PM	(3.18) H
9:16 AM	(3.66) H	3:45 PM	(1.15) L	8:55 PM	(2.90) H
10:10 AM	(3.59) H	4:57 PM	(1.34) L	9:44 PM	(2.56) H
11:09 AM	(3.43) H	6:18 PM	(1.48) L	10:45 PM	(2.21) H
12:19 PM	(3.24) H	7:57 PM	(1.48) L		
6:55 AM	(1.15) L	1:56 PM	(3.13) H	9:31 PM	(1.33) L
8:43 AM	(1.24) L	3:28 PM	(3.14) H	10:42 PM	(1.13) L
10:04 AM	(1.22) L	4:33 PM	(3.18) H	11:33 PM	(0.96) L
11:10 AM	(1.18) L	5:20 PM	(3.18) H		
6:02 AM	(2.63) H	12:02 PM	(1.17) L	5:56 PM	(3.14) H
6:39 AM	(2.79) H	12:47 PM	(1.21) L	6:25 PM	(3.06) H
7:11 AM	(2.91) H	1:25 PM	(1.28) L	6:50 PM	(2.95) H
7:41 AM	(3.00) H	1:58 PM	(1.37) L	7:13 PM	(2.83) H
8:09 AM	(3.05) H	2:28 PM	(1.45) L	7:31 PM	(2.70) H
8:36 AM	(3.08) H	2:58 PM	(1.54) L	7:50 PM	(2.58) H
9:03 AM	(3.07) H	3:30 PM	(1.62) L	8:11 PM	(2.46) H
9:33 AM	(3.04) H	4:10 PM	(1.70) L	8:35 PM	(2.33) H
10:08 AM	(2.98) H	5:00 PM	(1.78) L	9:01 PM	(2.20) H
10:48 AM	(2.89) H	6:04 PM	(1.84) L	9:33 PM	(2.06) H
11:37 AM	(2.80) H	7:45 PM	(1.84) L	10:19 PM	(1.91) H
12:37 PM	(2.73) H	9:24 PM	(1.72) I		
5:53 AM	(1.46) L	1:57 PM	(2.72) H	10:15 PM	(1.54) L
7:53 AM	(1.55) L	3:16 PM	(2.81) H	10:49 PM	(1.35) L
9:26 AM	(1.53) L	4:07 PM	(2.92) H	11:20 PM	(1.14) L
10:34 AM	(1.45) L	4:46 PM	(3.02) H	11:50 PM	(0.92) L
11:31 AM	(1.35) L	5:21 PM	(3.10) H		

TIDE TIMES

Tim Smith's

Townsville

POPULAR TIDE ADJUSTMENTS

Abbot Point	+40min
Cairns	+ 5min
Lucinda	0
Mackay Outer Harbour	+2hr 25min
Mourilyan Low tide	-15min
Mourilyan High tide	+5min
Port Douglas Low Tide	-20min
Port Douglas High Tide	0
Shute Harbour	+ 2hr 5min
Bowen	+ 35min
Cooktown	0
Flinders Reef	- 20min

Day	Date	Tide 1		
Mon	1	12:20 AM	(0.71)	L
Tue	2	12:49 AM	(0.52)	L
Wed	3	1:21 AM	(0.37)	L
THu	4	1:55 AM	(0.27)	L
Fri	5 ○	2:34 AM	(0.27)	L
Sat	6	3:18 AM	(0.36)	L
Sun	7	4:09 AM	(0.53)	L
Mon	8	5:05 AM	(0.78)	L
Tue	9	12:00 AM	(2.16)	H
Wed	10	1:40 AM	(2.08)	H
THu	11	3:25 AM	(2.15)	H
Fri	12	4:48 AM	(2.34)	H
Sat	13	5:50 AM	(2.56)	H
Sun	14	12:19 AM	(0.99)	L
Mon	15	12:48 AM	(0.94)	L
Tue	16	1:09 AM	(0.92)	L
Wed	17	1:23 AM	(0.90)	L
THu	18	1:36 AM	(0.86)	L
Fri	19	1:54 AM	(0.82)	L
Sat	20 ●	2:18 AM	(0.80)	L
Sun	21	2:47 AM	(0.81)	L
Mon	22	3:18 AM	(0.86)	L
Tue	23	3:52 AM	(0.96)	L
Wed	24	4:30 AM	(1.10)	L
THu	25	5:15 AM	(1.29)	L
Fri	26	1:06 AM	(2.07)	H
Sat	27	2:55 AM	(2.15)	H
Sun	28	4:25 AM	(2.41)	H
Mon	29	5:26 AM	(2.74)	H
Tue	30	6:15 AM	(3.09)	H
Wed	31	12:35 AM	(0.64)	L

DECEMBER 2025

Tide 2		Tide 3		Tide 4	
6:16 AM	(3.01) H	12:23 PM	(1.26) L	5:56 PM	(3.13) H
6:58 AM	(3.33) H	1:15 PM	(1.19) L	6:33 PM	(3.12) H
7:41 AM	(3.59) H	2:07 PM	(1.14) L	7:15 PM	(3.05) H
8:27 AM	(3.78) H	3:01 PM	(1.14) L	8:00 PM	(2.92) H
9:15 AM	(3.86) H	3:58 PM	(1.18) L	8:50 PM	(2.75) H
10:05 AM	(3.83) H	4:58 PM	(1.26) L	9:45 PM	(2.54) H
10:59 AM	(3.69) H	6:03 PM	(1.34) L	10:47 PM	(2.34) H
11:56 AM	(3.50) H	7:17 PM	(1.39) L		
6:13 AM	(1.06) L	1:00 PM	(3.28) H	8:34 PM	(1.37) L
7:43 AM	(1.31) L	2:15 PM	(3.09) H	9:48 PM	(1.29) L
9:14 AM	(1.47) L	3:29 PM	(2.97) H	10:53 PM	(1.18) L
10:35 AM	(1.55) L	4:30 PM	(2.88) H	11:42 PM	(1.07) L
11:46 AM	(1.57) L	5:17 PM	(2.80) H		
6:34 AM	(2.76) H	12:42 PM	(1.56) L	5:55 PM	(2.72) H
7:09 AM	(2.93) H	1:27 PM	(1.55) L	6:26 PM	(2.64) H
7:38 AM	(3.05) H	2:03 PM	(1.55) L	6:52 PM	(2.56) H
8:05 AM	(3.13) H	2:35 PM	(1.55) L	7:15 PM	(2.51) H
8:30 AM	(3.19) H	3:04 PM	(1.57) L	7:38 PM	(2.47) H
8:57 AM	(3.23) H	3:33 PM	(1.58) L	8:04 PM	(2.45) H
9:26 AM	(3.24) H	4:04 PM	(1.61) L	8:33 PM	(2.42) H
9:58 AM	(3.23) H	4:42 PM	(1.65) L	9:06 PM	(2.37) H
10:33 AM	(3.19) H	5:27 PM	(1.70) L	9:45 PM	(2.30) H
11:12 AM	(3.13) H	6:21 PM	(1.73) L	10:35 PM	(2.21) H
11:55 AM	(3.05) H	7:26 PM	(1.71) L	11:43 PM	(2.11) H
12:44 PM	(2.97) H	8:35 PM	(1.62) L		
6:25 AM	(1.51) L	1:41 PM	(2.89) H	9:38 PM	(1.46) L
8:17 AM	(1.69) L	2:46 PM	(2.83) H	10:30 PM	(1.26) L
10:01 AM	(1.73) L	3:53 PM	(2.80) H	11:15 PM	(1.04) L
11:30 AM	(1.66) L	4:49 PM	(2.79) H	11:56 PM	(0.84) L
12:37 PM	(1.51) L	5:40 PM	(2.80) H		
7:00 AM	(3.42) H	1:31 PM	(1.35) L	6:28 PM	(2.82)

POPULAR RIGS

Saltwater Rigs

Surface Float Rig

An excellent surface salmon rig consists of a styrene float, a couple of 4/0 hooks and a small sinker for weight. The hooks are tied on a metre or so of 15 kg monofilament trace and are spaced to hold a full pilchard comfortably. Slip a running ball sinker down the trace right on to the top hook. Then slip on a running styrene float and attach the top of the trace to a good quality swivel. This will allow the float to suspend your bait at the correct depth for feeding salmon. Should you require the bait to be set deeper, simply extend the trace length.

This rig casts reasonably well from a threadline or sidecast outfit and can be modified easily to suit small or large salmon, tommy ruff, tailor (with the inclusion of a light wire trace) and trevally.

Glitterbug float

Sinker

3–6 kg fluorocarbon leader to bait

5 kg mono

Fixed teardrop sinker

Freshwater Rig

Standard Paternoster for Boat and Bank

This is a standard rig for many Australian native species from barra to cod, using anything from a worm, to a yabby, to a live bait or prawn for barra.

You can vary the length of the droppers, depending on conditions, and the 3-way swivel could be substituted with a brass ring if the fish encountered are likely to pull your arms off! Add a red bead too—it can add a touch of spark and get those fish biting.

POPULAR KNOTS

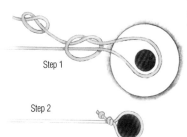

Step 1

Step 2

Arbor Knot

This is a very fast and secure knot for attaching line to the reel. Pass the tag end of the line around the spool and form an overhand knot with the tag end around the main line. Then another overhand knot on the tag end of the line. Lubricate the knots if using monofilament, tighten down by pulling the main line, and trim the tag.

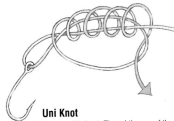

Uni Knot

An easy-to-tie versatile knot. Thread the eye of the hook with the line so the hook is suspended on a loop. Encircle the main line with the tag so another loop is formed. Wrap the double strand inside the loop with the tag. Make four wraps in all, leaving the tag protruding from the loop. Close the knot but do not pull it tight just yet. Slide the knot down onto the eye of the hook, pull it tight and trim the tag.

Homer Rhode Knot

This knot should never be used on lighter weight monofilaments, as it breaks at around 50 per cent of the line test.

1. Form an overhand knot in the main line leaving approximately 20 cm (8 inches) of monofilament between the knot and the tag end. Pass the tag end through the hook eye and then back through the overhand knot from the same side as it exited. Tighten the overhand knot lightly to the hook eye by pulling on the tail of the hook and on the tag end of the line, while keeping the two lines parallel to prevent the hook from twisting on the knot.

2. Make another overhand knot over the standing part of the line. This knot is the stopper for the loop, so its position determines the size of the loop, generally this knot would be 2–3 cm (1 inch) from the hook eye. Tighten this second knot and then pull on the bend of the hook and the main line at the same time.

3. The knot at the hook eye should slide up the line snugly into the second knot. Trim the tag.

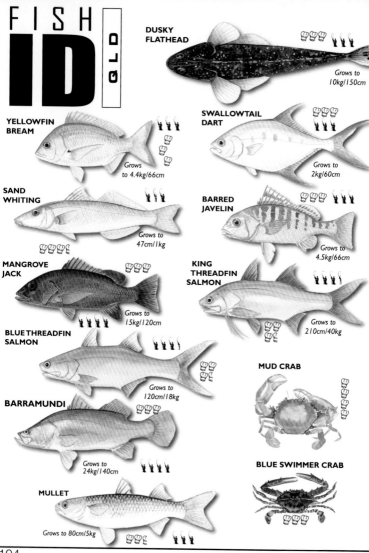

F I S H
ID
QLD

DUSKY FLATHEAD
Grows to 10kg/150cm

YELLOWFIN BREAM
Grows to 4.4kg/66cm

SWALLOWTAIL DART
Grows to 2kg/60cm

SAND WHITING
Grows to 47cm/1kg

BARRED JAVELIN
Grows to 4.5kg/66cm

MANGROVE JACK
Grows to 15kg/120cm

KING THREADFIN SALMON
Grows to 210cm/40kg

BLUE THREADFIN SALMON
Grows to 120cm/18kg

MUD CRAB

BARRAMUNDI
Grows to 24kg/140cm

MULLET
Grows to 80cm/5kg

BLUE SWIMMER CRAB

104

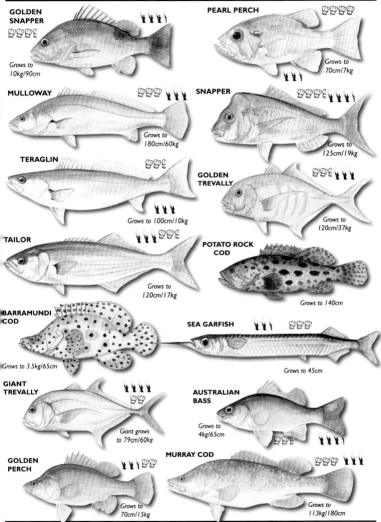

GOLDEN SNAPPER
Grows to
10kg/90cm

PEARL PERCH
Grows to
70cm/7kg

MULLOWAY
Grows to
180cm/60kg

SNAPPER
Grows to
125cm/19kg

TERAGLIN
Grows to
100cm/10kg

GOLDEN TREVALLY
Grows to
120cm/37kg

TAILOR
Grows to
120cm/17kg

POTATO ROCK COD
Grows to 140cm

BARRAMUNDI COD
Grows to 3.5kg/65cm

SEA GARFISH
Grows to 45cm

GIANT TREVALLY
Giant grows
to 79cm/60kg

AUSTRALIAN BASS
Grows to
4kg/65cm

GOLDEN PERCH
Grows to
70cm/15kg

MURRAY COD
Grows to
113kg/180cm

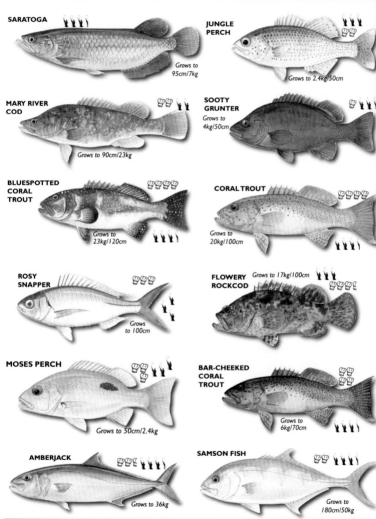

SARATOGA
Grows to 95cm/7kg

JUNGLE PERCH
Grows to 2.4kg/50cm

MARY RIVER COD
Grows to 90cm/23kg

SOOTY GRUNTER
Grows to 4kg/50cm

BLUESPOTTED CORAL TROUT
Grows to 23kg/120cm

CORAL TROUT
Grows to 20kg/100cm

ROSY SNAPPER
Grows to 100cm

FLOWERY ROCKCOD
Grows to 17kg/100cm

MOSES PERCH
Grows to 50cm/2.4kg

BAR-CHEEKED CORAL TROUT
Grows to 6kg/70cm

AMBERJACK
Grows to 36kg

SAMSON FISH
Grows to 180cm/50kg